The Braided Cord

The Braided Cord

THE STORY OF THE WILLIS FAMILY

—

Olive Martin Burns

ISBN-13: 9781544034454
ISBN-10: 1544034458
Library of Congress Control Number: 2017903366
CreateSpace Independent Publishing Platform
North Charleston, South Carolina

"We all come from the past, and children ought to know what it was that went into their making, to know that life is a braided cord of humanity stretching up from time long gone, and that it cannot be defined by the span of a single journey from diaper to shroud."
From: Baker, Russell, <u>GROWING UP. NEW YORK: CONGDON AND WEED, 1982. DISTRIBUTED BY ST. MARTIN'S PRESS, 1982.</u>
ACE BOOK TEXT

Dedication

"Stories have to be told or they die, and when they die we can't remember who we are or why we are here"
  Sue Monk Kidd THE SECRET LIVES OF BEES

I began to work on this story twenty years ago, and, now that I have about reached the end of my single journey, I think the time has come to put it in chronological, narrative form because this story cannot die—it must be told!

Somewhere in the 90's Richard Willis 111came to San Antonio on business, contacted me, and I invited him to come to our house for dinner. Lane Sealy, our cousin from the P.J. Willis branch of the family, lived near me, so I invited him to come along. Richard and Lane had been boyhood friends in Galveston, so they had many memories to share, as did I. We had a lively evening talking about the family. Richard told me that he had all of Mamie's letters, memorabilia, pictures, and extensive genealogical records, and asked if I would be interested in seeing them. Of course I was, so a couple of weeks later he appeared at my door with two huge banker's boxes full of papers. It took me many hours to go through them, decipher them, and get them organized. I persevered, made copies of everything, and returned the originals to Richard. He also gave me a copy of the story his Mom and Dad had written about the family. It is from these sources, combined with memories shared by my brothers and sisters, that this story has been compiled.

The story of the Willis family must live on in succeeding generations to give them a familiarity with the personalities who shaped us, admiration for the actions of some, a recognition of the faults of others, but overall a pride in the history of the family and the shared genes that bind them together. Hopefully knowing about our gene pool will help us to know who we are and why we are here.

Olive Elizabeth Martin Burns
April, 2017

Table of Contents

Acknowledgements

Our story covers four centuries (1700 – 2100) and seven generations, with a complicated cast of characters. I meander through the generations, digressing to tell the stories of the brothers in the fourth generation because this was the most exciting time of achievement and adventure.

Narcissa's family had to be included because her grandfather, Zachariah, was our first ancestor in Texas, and it was through her that we inherited the land in Montgomery.

Mamie's family, the Hawleys, were included because they so influenced her character and he was a prolific writer who so vividly told the story of his time.

Narcissa and Mamie deserved separate chapters because they drastically changed the coarse of our family history.

The notes of Richard 11 and Genevieve were a major source of insight into the family and relationships.

I am very indebted to my friend Don Michel, who generously shared his knowledge and computer skills.

I am also indebted to my many friends who patiently listened to me talk about this project, read the first crude copies, and offered suggestions, corrections, and encouragement.

This is my memorial to my mother whose name I bear, but of whom I have no memory.

CHAPTER 1

1ˢᵗ Generation

JOHN WILLIS 1

OUR STORY BEGINS WITH JOHN Willis. We know he was born in Wales because both his son and his two slaves state he came from Wales, saying he told them so. We do not know if he learned his blacksmithing trade in Wales and came to America as a land of opportunity, or perhaps came to America in the early 1700s as an indentured servant and learned his trade here. John settled in the Gum Island Swamps around Sussex County Delaware. He evidently prospered and was able to marry. Although the wife's name is unknown, she bore him three children, two boys and a girl. They owned two slaves, Aunt Illeka and Uncle Tom, who were raised in the house with his children and are the source of the little information we have.

The two sons were Joshua and Joseph, both becoming blacksmiths. The daughter, named Sallie, married a man named Pope, but was widowed early. She made her living spinning flax and wool.

CHAPTER 2

2ⁿᵈ Generation

JOHN WILLIS 11
ANN "NANA" SHORT

ON APRIL 13TH, 1745 SALLIE gave birth to a son, father unknown.

There could be many reasons why Sallie would not name the father of her child. Cousin "Hulda" (Mrs. Margaret Stevens) wrote "We have puzzled over this shortcoming. My sister suggests that he was the illegitimate child of Sallie Pope and was adopted by her father John. This happened across the street from me and she knew of a similar case. But we will never know, so why worry? Worse things have happened in families".

Sallie named her son John Willis.

Aunt Illeka and Uncle Tom tell the story of this John. In his boyhood he did a big turkey catching business until he was apprenticed to a blacksmith named Mulaney, to serve until he was 21. Mulaney kept him a year over his time as proved by his two older brothers, Joshua and Joseph Willis. (This would be 1767 and implies that John was, in the eyes of the court having jurisdiction over him, a legal brother, adopted by his grandfather). When young John learned his trade all his worldly goods consisted of a pair of leather britches and cowhide boots.

One year later, on June 6, 1768 John Willis married Ann "Nana" Short at The United Presbyterian Church in Lewis, Delaware.

They had six children: John, Arthur H, Mary (Polly), Eliza, Nancy and Short Adam.

John was a Revolutionary soldier, serving under a Captain Collins whose company was called "The Blue Hen's Chickens". In September 1777 John was wounded at the battle at Brandywine. His two brothers, Joshua and Joseph, were among the some 400 who died there. A month later John fought again at the battle at Germantown.

"Nana "died before John. His son Short wrote of his father "He courted all the widows but married none." John Willis died January 22ⁿᵈ, 1819 in Georgetown at age 69. His grandson, Arthur J., wrote" I saw the scars of his wounds when he was laid out. He died at our father's

(Short A. Willis') homestead and I saw his services for seven years in the army burnt up in Continental money and I have the old wallet that held it."

On November 2nd, 1817, two years before his death, John Willis wrote his Will. His oldest son John is not named in the Will. Cousin "Hulda" wrote "I think it is so bad we have always simply ignored John, the eldest son. I have never known about him, perhaps he was disinherited. Some were cut off without a shilling". Missing from the Will also is daughter Eliza. She married Joseph Ricketts (or Ricards) and must have died before the Will was written, but her son John Thomas Ricard is left one hundred dollars (the equivalent of $1,818.18 today). Both her brother Arthur H. and sister Nancy named a child after Eliza.

John left neither of the daughters any money in the Will, perhaps because he had given dowries when they married. Nancy married John Martin, an Englishman, and is left one bed and furniture, one carriage and harness, and one armed chair. Her daughter Eliza is (the equivalent to $1,818.18 today) and her son John is left his grandfather's set of blacksmith tools (we do not know if he became a blacksmith). Polly, who married John Spicer and had six children, is left one shilling "and no more of my estate". (There must be a story there!) The two sons, Arthur H. Willis and Short Adam Willis, were each left $484.50 which is the equivalent to $9,141.51 today, with the balance of the estate, after paying the legacies, debts, funeral charges, etc. to be divided equally between them. Short Adam Willis is named Executor.

John left a grand total of 25 grandchildren.

We cannot pursue each of these lives, though it is tempting with such notations as one "being killed in a mutiny on his own vessel in 1824, another "died of yellow fever in Brazil" and two brothers "being lost at sea in 1837". The one exception is the story of "The Silver Dollar Goddess", daughter of Arthur H. and John's great-granddaughter.

THE SILVER DOLLAR GODDESS

Morgan arrived in Philadelphia on October 9, 1876. His earliest pattern coins designed during his tenure at the Philadelphia Mint were intended for the half dollar. In 1876, Morgan enrolled as a student at the Pennsylvania Academy of the Fine Arts to prepare to create a new Liberty head design. Morgan also obtained studies from nature of the bald eagle for preparation of the reverse design. For the representation of Liberty, Morgan sought to depict an American woman rather than the usual Greek-style figures. Morgan's friend, artist Thomas Eakins, suggested he use Anna Willess Williams of Philadelphia as a model. In total, Morgan had five sittings with Williams; he declared her profile to be the most perfect he had seen. Van Allen, Leroy C.; Mallis, A. George (1991). *Comprehensive Catalog and Encyclopedia of Morgan & Peace Dollars*. Virginia Beach, Virginia: DLRC Press. ISBN 978-1-880731-11-6 Found on Wikepedia

Thomas Eakin was an American realist painter and art teacher. When his friend George Morgan was chosen to create the design for the new silver dollar that was to be minted at Philadelphia, he suggested that the model be a young teacher and former art student, the daughter of friends. Anna Willis Williams, the youngest of nine children, was 18 years old in 1876 and serving as the Principal of the Girl's School at The House of Refuge. She had to be persuaded to model and consented only with the assurance that her identity would not be revealed. Her obituary reads "When she became the model, Miss Williams was of medium height, graceful figure, complexion was fair, her eyes blue, her nose Grecian, and her hair, which was almost her crowning glory, was of golden color, abundant in quantity and light of texture, It was worn in a becoming soft coil."

The Morgan silver dollar was issued in 1878. Shortly thereafter Miss Williams ' identity was revealed in an article that appeared in <u>The Ladies Home Journal</u>. Miss Williams refused to talk about it, referring to it as "an incident of my youth.

Miss Williams served in the capacity of supervisor of kindergartens in the Philadelphia schools for 25 years, retiring in 1924 at the age of 66. Two years later she would die as the result of a broken hip. After her retirement Miss Williams issued a plea that kindergarten classes should be made compulsory on the grounds that it forms a keystone of the whole educational system. No doubt she would be pleased that in the twenty first century her plea has been answered.

In her obituary it is stated that Anna Willis Williams was the granddaughter of Dr. Arthur N. Willis. Mary Virginia Stevens, daughter of Col. Arthur John Willis, wrote" She was uncle

Arthur Willis' granddaughter". Anna would be the daughter of one of his two daughters, Eliza Anne or Mary Jane.

In a letter written in 1905 Mary Virginia Stevens also wrote "Alva Jones (another cousin) could give you Anna Williams' address, but I doubt very much if she will bother to write. I have always heard that she is very peculiar. Anyway, you might try. I have a history of Annie Williams but it is pasted in my scrapbook. If you write to The Ladies Home Journal, Phila. probably you might get a copy. I don't remember what year it was, but quite a while ago. I hope you can get it"

CHAPTER 3

3ʳᵈ Generation

———

SHORT ADAM WILLIS
MARY "POLLY" RICH

JOHN'S YOUNGEST SON AND OUR third generation, Short was born April 13ᵗʰ, 1783 in Sussex County, Delaware. At age 24 he married Mary "Polly" Rich of Bridgetown, Maryland on November 28ᵗʰ, 1812. "Polly" was the daughter of Peter Nixon Rich. "Hulda" wrote "Peter Nixon Rich served in The Revolutionary War as an officer in the regiment led by his first wife's brother, Col. Wm. Whitely. Peter was afterwards a member of the legislature and was carried on a sailboat in a featherbed to Annapolis to vote, there being a tie in the House. His vote put down negro suffrage. That proved to be his death's sickness, and he was buried at Annapolis. Mary "Polly" Rich was the daughter by Peter's second wife Prudence Lane.*

Short Adam and "Polly" had eight children. The family bible records the births thus:

1. Arthur John Willis borned September 17ᵗʰ, 1813.
2. Peter James was born on Easter Sunday; which was March the 24ᵗʰ, 1815.
3. Sarah Ann was born January the 12ᵗʰ, 1817. Departed this life September the 24ᵗʰ, 1828.
4. WIlliam H. Willis was born July the 14ᵗʰ, 1819. Died July the 2ⁿᵈ 1843 in his 24ᵗʰ year.
5. Richard Short was borned October the 17ᵗʰ, 1821.
6. Thomas Alexander was borned October the 17ᵗʰ, 1822.
7. Mary Ellen was borned June 11ᵗʰ about midnight (1824)
8. Not recorded in the bible, but listed by family members is the 8ᵗʰ child, Mary Elizabeth, who died at age 4.

It seems certain that Short farmed for a living. He inherited from his father we know, and since his wife came from a prominen t family, it is safe to assume that she came into the marriage with a dowry.

Short and his two brothers, Arthur H. and John Jr., joined with others to defend their area from the British in the War of 1812, being present at the bombardment of Lewistown (now Lewes, Delaware) on April 6ᵗʰ and 7ᵗʰ, 1813.

Two years after his father died in 1822, the couple moved to the Willis homestead, near Georgetown, Delaware. As early as 1838 they were receiving mail at Caroline County, Maryland. Short Adam Willis was awarded the Royal Arch Degree, the climax of Ancient Craft Masonry and Masonic Symbolism.

Of their five boys and three girls Short and "Polly" lost two of their girls early on: Sarah Ann died in 1828 at age 11 and Mary Elizabeth died at age four. Mary Ellen, the baby of the family grew up with five brothers who, according to family legend, adored her.

Margaret Sealy Burton wrote "Mary Ellen was the only daughter whom the boys worshiped. She was badly spoilt and quite determined. During the time their roof was being renovated, she fell in love with the Scot carpenter who worked on the job. Failing to convince her parents of her determination to marry him, she crept out of her bedroom window and escaped on a ladder he had placed against the side of the roof and they eloped. The boys were so broken hearted without her at home that they decided to leave for Texas". The Scot Mary Ellen eloped with was named James A. Jones. They had one son named Alva B. Jones. Mary Ellen died in 1879. It is thought her son Alva Jones had possession of the family bible. Both Peter and Richard named a daughter in honor of this adored little sister.

Although we know little of the details of Short and Polly lives, we know that they built a strong and lasting bond in their family that was carried on in the next generation between their surviving children, a legacy more valuable than any inheritance of worldly goods. From the letters the sons in Texas wrote to their parents back in Maryland we sense the love and loyalty shared by all.

In a letter from Houston, Texas dated January, 1838 Peter wrote "I can only say in this that they (the boys) are very much pleased with thare exchange. I will attend to thare writing to you as well as myself. I have nothing more at present, but read this to my dear Mother and tell her the boys have listened to my advice as a Father, been obedient as brothers when we talked of her we shed tears of affection together. In short my soul has been a pleasure given but wishing to my only brother & little sister & to all my inquiring friends as to if we should ever meet again. I hope we may never part in a flood of tears as we did at Arthur John's, which I never, never, never, never shall forget. I remain your son, Peter J. Willis

In a letter from Washington-on-the-Brazos, dated July 2, 1838 Peter wrote "I have been absent from the boys two months but soon found way to them after selling out, and found them both well. I think your first letter is there and they informed me they had written to you and informed you of how they are doing. Thare corn is latter but flourishing. Richard commenced work with the gentleman he boarded with the morning I left – William is to finish plowing the corn over for the last time and then go to work also by this means to work out thare board. They are very well pleased with that settlement where they are and Will talked about if he and Dick had a piece of land of thare own in that settlement he would ask no man any add, so thare was a sale of land while I was thare but was sold in lotts than they want but one of thare neighbors bought a lot & told me I could have two hundred acres for them for the same he gave and the same payments which was two dollar per acre one to cash balance in payments that I willingly agreed to as I was anxious for them to settle also. I knew it would be a gratification to you for them to have a home of thare own, and as this land that I shall locate will be on the frontier where it is not safe to settle as yet – I tole them not to take the land until thare part was designated.

I am very glad to hear from my dear sister, that she still commemorates her brothers' birthday, which gratitude I know they will repay.

Dear Mother and Father I remain your ornery son Peter J. Willis

In a letter dated June 28, 1839, mailed from Houston, Texas and addressed to Short Adam Willis, Caroline County, Maryland, Hunting Creek, PR Peter wrote "I hope you will continue to write regular and I will try and not be so neglectful of writing as I have been. Tell Arthur to write also for I had much rather pay 37ct. for a letter than go to the theater. I am very happy to hear of my Mother's enjoying good health, and still attending her meetings where I know she enjoys herself so well among her old acquaintances * but that remedy she has found for rheumatic pains is very simple but I fear she will exercise too much knowing as I do that she believes in it so strong. William and Richard's best wishes to Mother & family also to our absent sister and tell her to write to me. I remain your affectionate son Peter J Willys P.S. I am very glad to hear of the conclusion you and Mother have come to that it is sending Mary to a good school and there keep her if your circumstances will admit – of rite she accomplishes her education."

In a letter written from Montgomery on January 3rd, 1846 signed by "your affectionate son P.J. Willis "Richard talks a good deal of marrying but has not done it yet. We have had quite a Merry Christmas a given many parties & of a profusion, an address by the Masons on Sunday last from a lodge at this place. I tell Caroline if we don't make better collections than the present prospects bid fair it will be uncertain about her going with me home next summer. She is anxious for to see you all. Our boy (William Henry Willis, born December 7, 1845) has been quite sick with worms but is well again and running all about – will be thirteen months old on the 7th of this month and outcries a camp meeting. Caroline thinks a woman can't keep her matters well regulated about her house without getting mad at least once a month, and she wants to know of Mother if she is not reasonable enough. She has not been mad this year so far.

Dear Parents: You may infer from Mr. Willis that I was always mad but Mother you know we will get vexed about our little house matters, but Mr. Willis is of so even a temper himself he thinks I should never get in a bad humour though I think we get along very well. Sister

Mary you must write often as I am always glad to hear from you and must excuse me for not writing to you before as I am so poor a hand to write but I will try to write to you oftener. Mr. Willis speaks of taking me with him to see you all next summer but I tell him I am afraid that it will be inconvenient for me to leave home so long as we have just got under way of keeping house though I should be very glad to see you and take our little boy to see his grandparents. I shall insist on Mr. Willis going if I don't as he has not been home so long and talks about you all so much. Give my love to sister Caroline and brother John (she refers here to brother Arthur John Willis and his wife Caroline Hutchinson) from his letter we expected him out this fall but I tell Mr. Willis and brother that none of you will come to this backwoods country. I hope we may hear from you often. I remain your affectionate daughter Caroline Willis Your affectionate son Peter J. Willis

Dear Parents: I join in as third and last in this letter to you and all of the family but feeling quite unwell this last month from colds that have settled in my chest, but sincerely hoping we will hear from you and sister.

    Your affectionate son R.S. Willis

William H. Willis died in the Yellow Fever epidemic in 1843. Margaret Sealy Burton wrote "My father George Sealy, and William Henry were devoted friends. Both were taken desperately ill and lay side-by-side. William Henry died and it was several weeks later before they dared to break the sad news to my father."

Charles W. Hayes, in his book <u>Galveston, History of the Island and the</u> City wrote "The happy unity that had existed between the three brothers, who labored as one man for the common purpose, was suddenly broken in July, 1843, by the death of William H., who fell a victim to the malaria of the Brazos bottoms. This was a trying blow to the surviving brothers."

The last letter to the parents was written from Montgomery April 26, 1850.

    "Dear Parents We have had no letter from you for some time but have had several from Thomas & which have mentioned you both and we are glad to hear of your good health. Father mentioned in one of Thomas' letters the hardship it was to him to write on account of the tremor in his hand, which we suppose is the reason for not having a letter direct from you. Thomas wrote to us when he returned from Ireland that his next trip would probably be to California and I wrote him of he should ever leave you again that I should insist on his visiting us though I have never insisted on any of my relatives visiting us in Texas and particular Thomas the last remaining child with you. I could not think of requesting him or advising him ever to leave you – but if it is his intention with your consent to leave that country for any other I shall insist and both our families do the same that he visit us and look at this country for himself and as we have before said if he likes and wishes to engage in business of any kind we would be ready and willing to help him. Give our love to our sister Mary Ellen and her husband and tell them we would be glad to hear from them and keep up a correspondence with them. Accept our kindest wish for your good health and prosperity and give our love to all enquiring friends. To our affectionate parents P.J. Willis & Brother

The youngest brother, Thomas, did accept the invitation and came to Texas.

Arthur John Willis, in a letter written to his brother Richard S, Willis on April 19, 1878 wrote: "I was just looking over my list and see that Uncle Thomas' name is not there, and for fear it was not written I will tell you. He was the youngest child. Left here for Texas in 1851 and died in Galveston and is buried in the Citizens' burying ground."

Short died November 6th, 1860, followed by "Polly" on September 15th, 1861. At the time of their deaths they were living on the Short A. Willis farm near Preston. Maryland. They were married 48 years and had 27 grandchildren.

On January 1, 1861 Peter wrote to his brother Arthur: "You did not say whether Mother had broken up housekeeping or not. I will send your letter to Richard. I have no objection to selling the land alluded and perhaps he has none if you and Mother think best."

Some ten years later the three boys ordered a monument for Short and Polly. Richard was in Maryland overseeing this project together with brother Arthur J. Peter's instructions were "I do think I would get just as large a monument as could get on the ground regardless of a few dollars." He mentions services, so it could be there was a dedication ceremony of some sort. The monument:

Short A. Willis
Born April 13th 1783
Died Nov. 6 1860
Mary Willis
Wife of Short A. Willis
Born June 24' 1788
Died Sept. 15' 1861

"The above was found on the old Short Willis farm near Preston, Maryland.
Signed: Mrs. Howard Harris,
Preston, Maryland Comm. Chairman of old cemeteries in Caroline County."

CHAPTER 4

4th Generation

——

ARTHUR JOHN WILLIS
CAROLINE HUTCHINSON

TEN MONTHS AFTER THEY WERE married Short Adam and Polly welcomed their first child, a boy, whom they named Arthur John. "As a boy he worked on his father's farm in Dorchester County. At age 20 he went north and sailed from Boston on the brig Franklin. After that he visited every seaport of note in the United States. He was for a long time engaged in the freighting business, and built the "Mary Willis", a large sailing vessel. In 1835 he engaged in the lumber business and succeeded by dint of hard work in paying for several tracts of land near the Choptank River."

From The Denton (Maryland) Journal.

In 1839, at the age of 26, he married the widow Caroline Hutchison, two years older than he and described by the Denton Journal as "a most estimable lady of Dorchester County". They had a family of five children, but lost their only son in infancy, one daughter at age 5 and another at age 35.

Margaret Sealy Burton, a great niece of Arthur James Willis, has written a character study of this couple: "Caroline – austere, narrow minded, good housekeeper – making preserves – keeping house dark and gloomy to keep out flies – refused a summer trip to White Mountains as my grandfather's guest because she had to dry out her apples. He offered to buy her a whole barrel of apples, but she said they would never taste as good as hers.

Arthur John, her husband, went to Boston to buy a new suit of clothes and came home with the tails of his broadcloth coat to his heels. Said the tailor said it didn't cost any more and he thought it would please his parsimonious, economical better half. He wore it to shreds, even while State Senator. He also had a black satin waistcoat with a large silver button on it.

He was the jolliest man in Maryland and for the amusement of his children he would lay on the floor and wallow like a menagerie. He always wore red flannel underwear for his underclothes as he suffered from rheumatism and one day in one of these evolutions his trouser seat popped open and yards of red flannel came bursting out to the embarrassment of the old gentleman and the hilarity of the children. Arthur John was an avid speaker "against the delay to call a Convention to form a new Constitution – in support of the Constituti0on, the Restoration of the Union and the faithful maintenance of the Laws, - and in keeping and preserving inviolate the Purity and Supremacy of the White Race."

In 1847 Arthur John purchased the estate of General William Potter known as Potters Landing, changing the name to Williston. During his ownership it was the leading shipping point in Caroline County with sailing vessels for trade to Baltimore.

He traveled extensively in the United States and in Europe. He was commissioned a Colonel by the governor in 1861, serving with the 93rd Pennsylvania volunteers. In 1849 he was elected to the State Senate, serving a term of 6 years. In 1864 he was elected to the State Senate, this time on the Union ticket. In 1866 he was elected to The House of Delegates. He ran again in 1874, but was defeated.

Writing of her father "Hulda" said" he was elected to the Senate in 1862 at which time he made a thrilling speech called "Thunder and Lightening". It was classed with Abraham Lincoln's - was printed in gilt letters on blue paper." His verbosity is a trait that surfaces in later generations. Caroline Hutchinson Willis died in March, 1873. Arthur John and Caroline had been married 34 years. They are survived by two daughters, Mary Virginia Stevens, called "Hulda", and Caroline Sophia Messick, and 15 grandchildren.

In 1875 Arthur married for the second time to Miss Belle Rawlings, the daughter of his second cousin. They were married 14 years before his death in 1889.

PETER JAMES WILLIS
CAROLINE WOMACK

P J WILLIS

MAGNOLIA WILLIS SEALY

Born on Easter Sunday, March 26, 1815 in Caroline County, Maryland, the second son of Short Adam and Polly Willis, and just 22 months younger than his brother Arthur J., Peter grew up on his father's farm. Following the lead of Arthur, who left the farm in 1833 to go north and explore the world, Peter left in 1836 to go south, joining the many who had GTT - "gone to Texas". He came with trading on his mind. In that first visit of six months, he became very aware of certain shortages in the region.. When he returned in 1837, with his two younger brothers William Henry and Richard, he brought provisions to sell. In a letter of January, 1838 he wrote" When I left Baltimore I bought sundry of articles to the amount of $100, which I did not inform you of as I thought it was time when I sold them. I also bought purvisions in Orleans to the amount of $100, which I have sold at 100 per cent – after I sold my purvisions, which consisted of Butter & Cheese, they became low – I then laid out my money in the same articles. Purvisions are now getting high again. After all the narrow escapes & misfortunes we have been fortunate, with what money we have now & putting the things I have now on hand at the lowest price "we will have $100 more than the day we left home clear of passage to this place & other expenses on the way which was $200."

The three Willis boys settled in Houston, surviving by going into the wood business supplying wood for the steamships, building houses and doing odd jobs. Peter, as the older brother, counseled his two brothers and kept watch over them. He remained in Houston, where he could wheel and deal, at the same time traveling extensively through Texas to size up the possibilities. The boys went first to Washington, doing agricultural work and eventually buying land on the road from Navasota to Washington.

"After a year or two Peter J. made his first entry into the mercantile world in Houston, then buying a stock of goods and opening a store in Washington. The two brothers remained on the farm until the death of William Henry, when Richard S. joined Peter J. in business, the brothers locating their joint mercantile venture at Montgomery." (From Indian Wars and Pioneers Of Texas, by John Henry Brown, E. Daniel, Publisher, Austin, Texas)

An ad in the Montgomery Patriot dated July 2, 1845 states "Just received and will constantly keep on hand a general assortment of DRY GOODS and GROCERIES" P. J. Willis & Brother

Peter married Caroline Womack on January 21, 1845. He was 30 and she was 18. They had a family of six children, two boys and four girls.

"Peter J. was five feet eleven and half inches in height, weighing 185 pounds, dark, sandy hair, florid complexion, grey eyes, of a buoyant, social, convivial temperament. He was a man of unlimited resources, abounding in good humor, with a repertoire of personal anecdotes, which he related in an inimitable manner and with telling effect. His relationship with acquaintances and friends was that of the heartiest good fellowship."

(From Galveston, History of The Island and the City, Volume 2, by Charles W. Hayes)

Mr. Willis possessed many of the elements of popularity and easily won and readily retained the friendship of those with whom he came in contact. He was genial by nature, kind in disposition, and easily approached. He cherished an especially warm feeling for his associates of early days and was fond of recounting with them his early experiences in Texas. He was devoted to the State of his adoption and to all of its interests and institutions and lost no opportunity to show his attachment. He was not a member of any church, but was a liberal contributor to all, owned pews in all the churches in the city and, in fact, gave of his ample means to all worthy purposes. He never held a public office, but lent his name and the aid of a strong personal example to the side of the law, order, and good government, and occupied a number of positions in connection with the business interests of the several localities of the State in which he was at one time or another a resident. (From Indian Wars and Pioneers of Texas by John Henry Brown, L.E. Daniell, Publisher, Austin, Texas.)

In 1845 Peter built a Greek Revival two-story frame home in Montgomery, naming it for his daughter, Magnolia. In his letter to his parents of January, 3.1846 Peter wrote "We have had quite a Merry Christmas a given many parties & of a profusion". "The house was completed in time for the Willis family to throw a large Christmas party that boasted Montgomery's first Christmas tree. "Magnolia" was often the scene for many festive occasions and it is said that Sam Houston, a personal friend of Willis was a frequent houseguest whenever he went bear hunting at nearby Bear Bend, a favorite spot for this sport." (From "Historic Homes" by Bill Bancroft "Montgomery: A tradition of gracious Southern Living": Texas Home Magazine)

That home still stands today, complete with many of the original furnishings, and is included in the annual heritage tour.

Caroline Willis "was a woman of rare judgment and good practical sense, whose devotion to her husband and children, coupled with her kindly, sympathetic nature endeared her to all who came within its well directed influence"

(From Galveston – History of the Island and the City, Volume 2, by Charles W. Hayes)

"She was a woman of most exemplary character, and not a little of the success which her husband achieved was attributable to the inspiration that emanated from her noble life." (From Indian Wars and Pioneers of Texas, by John Henry Brown)

"Caroline Willis, wife of P.J. Willis, departed this life on the 19 September, 1863 at Belton in her 36 year. She was fully prepared to die and hailed death as a welcome messenger to relieve her of her sufferings of a lingering illness which had prayed upon her for more than four years. Her prayers were answered by the arrival of her husband some fifteen hours before her death. She is being removed to Montgomery. She leaves a husband and six children to mourn her". From the Willis family bible.

Only a year later daughter Tabitha Willis died at age 16. The other three daughters, Ella, Magnolia, and Caroline, were sent to boarding school in New York, while Peter and his two sons, Peter J., Jr. and William H., went to the office in Brownsville. The Montgomery house and contents were sold.

Magnolia Willis returned to Galveston from boarding school to marry George Sealy, twenty years older than she. A business associate of her father, this same George Sealy was the best friend of her uncle William who died in the Malaria epidemic of 1843. Family lore is that her bachelor brother-in-law named his oil company for her, The Magnolia Petroleum Company, which later became The Mobil Oil Company. Magnolia died in 1933 at the age of 79.

Peter and Caroline had fifteen grandchildren.

Peter married a second time to a Miss Harriet Aiken from New York. He suffered for some years with digestive problems, and died in 1873 at age 58 while on a business trip to Kansas City.

RICHARD SHORT WILLIS

R.S WILLIS

Born in 1821, the fourth of five sons, Richard's life was greatly influenced by his brothers. The oldest two boys were very assertive, adventurous young men. Richard was more reserved. He lived the first 16 years of his life on the farm, learning lessons of family loyalty, obedience and responsibility.

Richard watched as older brother Arthur left the farm to venture north to explore the world on the sea. Next he saw older brother Peter join the many who had GTT – "gone to Texas" to explore the possibilities of that land to the south. When Peter returned with glowing reports of opportunities for land and growth in that newly developing territory, Richard 16 and William 18, were eager for the adventure. Leaving the family "in a flood of tears", they and Peter joined a caravan of neighbors to ride horseback to Texas in 1837. Settling in the bayou city of Houston, they scrambled to eke out a living, doing whatever jobs they could find – farming chores, cutting wood, building houses – being paid $2.50 per day each and boarded, Peter always in the lead, William and Richard working side-by-side as a team. Peter wrote that the boys "have listened to my advice as a father and been obedient as brothers".

When they ran out of work they became "verry orneary" as they were paying $8.00 a week board. Peter gave them a letter to his acquaintance, a Mr. Morrell, and on December

28th of 1837 the two boys left for Washington, about 60 miles north of Houston. William found work with a farmer at Grocery Retreat, about 15 miles before Washington, at $25 a month. Richard proceeded to Washington and was hired on by Mr. Morrell. Peter continued to travel around the territory, exploring possibilities.

After two months away Peter returned to check on the boys and found them both well. They indicated to him that they would like to purchase land in that area and settle there permanently. William wrote a letter dated February 17, 1839 telling how he and Richard went into partnership with Peter and a Mr. Hicks in Houston supplying wood for the steamships, were able to make enough money to buy the land they wanted. Peter, who had opened a small store in Houston, now moved his store to Washington to be near his brothers.

The Brazos River area is very hot and humid. Various diseases were rampant. William writes of "yellow ganders" (which could be yellow jaundice or hepatitis), Peter writes of "Billory fever" which might be another name for Malaria, and then there was "Yellow Fever", of which there was an epidemic in 1843-44. Peter, ever the entrepreneur, writes of "helping sick persons – the usual dose from forty – 150 grains of colomil, then followed by a dose of castor oil and all the cold water they can drink- ice is recommend. I bought the medicine and administered it myself. The rate of charges is $5.00 for each visit - $1.00 per nite and double mileage at nights".

In July 1839 brother William came down with yellow fever and died. "The happy unity that had existed between the three brothers, who had labored as one man, for one common purpose, was suddenly broken. This was a trying blow to the surviving brothers". (From Galveston, The History of the Island and the City", Vol. 2, Charles W. Hayes)

Within a couple of years the two surviving brothers moved their mercantile partnership P.J. Willis & Bro. to Montgomery, a more northerly, central location, and in direct line with Houston and Galveston, leaving behind their heartbreak and making a fresh start. By 1845 the store was open, as evidenced by an ad placed in The Montgomery Patriot, date July 2. 1845:" Just received and will constantly keep on hand, a general assortment
    DRY GOODS and GROCERIES
    P. J. Willis & Bro."
    In a letter dated January 3, 1846 Peter wrote to his father "Richard talks a gooddeal of marrying but has not done it yet". Richard 11 and Gen write about a first marriage. "R.S. Willis was married for the first time to a Montgomery girl (name unknown) who died of T.B. She was only 16 at her death and had no children. He built a home, and filled it with imported furniture from England which came by ship to Galveston and to Montgomery by mule cart. The house was very slow to completion. During this time the young Mrs. Willis' health grew progressively worse. Among the items Mrs. Willis particularly craved was a bathtub. This, at the

time, was a decided status symbol, as most everyone bathed in a tin washtub. In those days bathtubs were made of tin with a hardwood ledge fashioned around the outer edge. The finest were made in England. Mrs. Willis, being young, felt very deprived that the tub was so long in transit. Unfortunately, she died the day before the treasure arrived in Montgomery. Her grieving husband uncrated the bathtub and was delighted with its beauty. It was light blue with pink water lilies painted on the outside. Knowing how his wife had longed for this English luxury, he ignored the traditional coffin and buried her in the bathtub."

At first I dismissed this as a romantic concoction from the imaginations of Richard and Gen, as I could find no record of this marriage or any gravesite for this young bride buried in the bathtub. However, several known facts have made me reconsider. Peter wrote in January, 1846 "Richard "talks a gooddeal of marriage" but it was not until a good year and a half later that he married Narcissa Worsham, ample time to bury the first wife and go through the grieving process. E.B. Stewart, in a letter to Mamie, wrote" My wife says that she thinks the old family bible was burned at the time that the Mr. R.S. Willis ' house was burned in Montgomery sometime before the Civil War". Narcissa and Richard were married seven years before J. S. Shelton built their house in 1854. The house that burned must have been their home for those seven years. Could this be the house that Richard 1built for the young bride? Was the record of that first marriage burned up with the bible? Mamie, for all her meticulous genealogical record keeping and investigation, makes no mention of her husband Short's first two marriages, only brought to light by a letter from a relative. I have concluded that the story of the "light blue bathtub with pink water lilies painted on the sides" could possibly be true — lost through the passage of time.

Built in Montgomery in 1854, the Richard Willis house is a registered Texas historical site, now a bed and breakfast.

Richard 1 was very busy with the continually growing business and frequent business traveling. "It was characteristic of Richard Willis, however, to be a veritable giant in business, accustomed to making decisions quickly, he concerned himself little with "trifling details", as he called them. I recall one instance when I was with Mr. Willis in their cotton sampling room. A Greek buyer from the firm of Ralli Bros. entered to trade with Mr. Willis on a very large consignment of cotton. There was some discussion as to whether the price per pound should be 14 ¼ or 14 1/8, the Greek holding out for the latter. Mr. Willis turned to the Greek saying "My friend, my clerks here are too busy to make out an account sales in eighths. I shall flip this silver dollar; if it comes up heads, you pay me 14 ¼, if tails you may have the cotton at 14 1/8. It was agreed and the coin flipped. In keeping with Mr. Willis' usual luck, the coin fell heads up and the trade, involving 250 bales went through at 14 ¼.

During the period when R.S. Willis was vice-President of Santa Fe Railroad he called me into his office one day and told me that I was not to take a vacation that year, explaining that he had just sold the Santa Fe 5,000,000 feet of lumber, with the privilege of increasing the order 5,000,000 more. I had been delegated to receive the lumber from Calcasieu and other mills in Louisiana, render the account sales and have the amounts credited to the various mills that they might use the funds for further purchases of commodities from Willis & Bro. It required five months to accomplish this task, upon the completion of which I was given a bonus of $500 in lieu of my vacation." (From <u>Lives of the Willis Brothers</u>, The Houston Chronicle, October, 1936.)

"He (Richard S. Willis) was an indefatigable worker all his life and not until physical infirmities obtained mastery over his iron will was he able to pull against the current of his earlier days. He served in various positions of trust and his name was connected from first to last with many corporate enterprises in the city. He was President of The Galveston National Bank, having brought the affairs of its predecessor, The Texas Banking and Insurance Company, to a successful termination. He was one of the promoters of the Gulf, Colorado and Santa Fe Railway and, for some years a member of its Directory. He was Chairman of the Deep Water Committee, a prominent member of The Cotton Exchange and of the Chamber of Commerce; President of The Texas Guarantee & Trust Company, and a member of the Directory of the Southern Cotton Press & Manufacturing Company. Mr. Willis was devoted to business and no man ever left his affairs in better shape or knew more about the details of every enterprise with which he was connected."

"Until ill health compelled him to desist, his personal supervision, judgment and valuable experience were given entirely to the affairs and details of the business. He was rather of a reserved disposition and of marked individuality. He was possessed of strong prejudices either for or against measures and men, but withal generous and confiding where such feelings were required. He was a man of the greatest perseverance and will power, and possessed of strict business ideas to the greatest extent" (From <u>Indian Wars and Pioneers of Texas</u> by John Henry Brown.)

"R.S. Willis always wore a "two-story" beaver hat – the remainder of his immaculate ensemble completing his picturesque appearance." (Both Kate and Mamie objected to this description - Kate wrote "The picture he draws of Father is really funny – purely imaginary on his part.") Mr. Willis never lost his taste for farming and, while yet a merchant prince, he bought for his own use the historic Darrington plantation of 1830 acres near Sandy Point. Here he installed a sugar mill at a cost of $150,000 dollars and introduced for the first time in Texas the present method of sugar refining and manufacturing, and also provided facilities for handling the corn, sugar and cotton crops of his neighbors, including a narrow-gage tram road for transporting commodities to and from his plantation. The Darrington Plantation originally had been the home of Sterling McNeil, one of Stephan F. Austin's first 300 and is now one of the state's finest farms.

At the age of 80, still sturdy and active, Mr.Willis, with his long, white beard flowing to the winds, would mount his Kentucky thoroughbred and set out for the plantation. My last sight of him, on one of these occasions, was on Main Street in Houston - on route to his farm. His palatial residence still stands on Broadway in Galveston.

Richard Short Willis was a distinguished citizen of Texas and the Old South, a constructive dreamer who literally made dreams come true and who helped right nobly and well to build the region in which he lived."(From <u>Lives of the Willis</u> Brothers by J. A, Ziegler)

Richard Short Willis died July 26, 1892 in Manitou Springs, Colorado. His wife Narcissa was by his side.

NARCISSA WORSHAM

MRS. R. S. WILLIS.

Narcissa's monument now the Moody Mansion Museum

On June 3, 1847 Richard married Narcissa Worsham, sixth child of Jeremiah and Katherine Landrum Worsham. (It is through Katherine that we claim our first ancestor in Texas, Zachariah Landrum, who arrived in 1829 as one of the original "300" to settle with Stephan F. Austin) For the first seven years of her life she was the only girl with four older brothers. The Mary E. Davis Collection in the Genealogy Department of the Montgomery County Library states of Narcissa "She had vivid memories of coming in a wagon from Alabama as a small child. to Texas". That same year a little sister, Elizabeth, was born, and four years another sister, Letitia. Narcissa was 19 when she married Richard. Their first son Short Adam was born July 3, 1848. Thus began, for Narcissa, a series of childbirths spanning twenty-five years. In that time she gave birth to ten children, starting at age 20 and giving birth to that last child when she was 45. This period of her life was shadowed by death – her mother died when Narcissa was 24, she lost her third child (a son named Richard) infancy. Three of her pregnancies resulted in stillbirths, those babies buried without markers in their grandfather's burial ground. In order the surviving children were: Short Adam, 1848, Katherine, 1853, Anna Laura, 1860, Lee, 1863, Richard Martin, 1868, and Beatrice Olive, 1873.

Their Montgomery home was built in 1854. They lived in that home until 1862, when they moved to Houston, then on to Galveston in 1868. In 1871/72 they purchased the house on Broadway, their family home until Richard's death.

"Richard, in a letter to his parents dated January, 1854 writes "Narcissa is fat" (possibly pregnant?). He hints at her demanding personality. In a letter of 1854 Richard wrote "Narcissa made me promise the first thing after my return never to leave home again or even think of it – but since then it may be necessary that I should & I have commenced talking before her of going next summer & I think if it should be necessary for me to go she would give her consent".

In August 1855 Richard wrote his brother Arthur" I stopped at Father's with Narcissa. She will visit with your family before you return. I have one particular request to make of you – will you quit work to some extent & go with your wife and mine to some camp meeting or meetings & try if possible to make Narcissa enjoy herself – being among strangers and of a backward and timid disposition & I am afraid she will become dissatisfied & write to me to come after her – try to prevent this if possible."

It was written of Narcissa that she "led an eminently domestic life". While the husband, who spent his entire life playing second fiddle to his older brother Peter (and happily so), buried himself in his work, and had his interest in Darrington plantation for relaxation, Narcissa was at home, often pregnant, managing the household, seeing to the education of the children, and traveling at times with her husband. She often went to New York to be with the girls.

Richard and Narcissa were married for 45 years. In 1892, at age 64, she became a widow, and in control of an enormous fortune. She had watched as George and Magnolia Sealy built their mansion, designed by Stanford White, the New York architect, a project that took three years, being completed in 1889.

"Architecture in the late nineteenth and early twentieth centuries provided the means by which railroad, cotton and cattle barons could display their wealth and success" (From Alexander, Drury B., Texas Homes of the Nineteenth Century, University of Texas Press, (Austin and London)

Narcissa tore down the home in which she and her husband had lived for some twenty years and where they had raised their family, and replaced it with a 31- room mansion with a square footage of 27,400.5 at an estimated cost of $125,000.00 (roughly three million in 2015).

"She (Narcissa) decided to tear down their house and build a monument to her taste and cultural refinement. She did not want a dowager cottage or a tasteful carpenter's gothic fantasy. It was her desire to build a mansion that would outshine all the other houses that lined Broadway". (From the archives of the Moody Museum,)

She chose as her architect William H. Tyndall, "largely a designer of industrial buildings and fire stations", who created a house that was modern in many ways."

" With the exception of the curved west side of the mansion, the texture of the red brick walls is uniformly flat, broken only by the limestone trim. The cornice moldings and window trim are relatively plain. While the rounded arches and massive character of the house suggest the Romanesque style, the design is quite simple. Each of the three towers is different in shape – round, square, octagonal – but none offers any surprises. The towers, all of the same scale and height, seem to counteract each other.

Convenience was a premium concern in Mrs. Willis' household. The ground floor basement had butler's quarters, a furnace room, a storage room for coal, a water heater for the conservatory, an elevator, a dumbwaiter, and a "clothes dryer" that circulated hot air from a stove over clothing racks. Structural steel was used to help support the floors – a first for houses in Texas. Also at ground level is a porte cochere with ornamental ironwork. The noted firm of Portier & Stymus of New York designed the interiors. African Mahogany, white oak, cherry, birch, and bird's eye maple are among the fine woods used for the interior finish. The dining room is 26 ft. wide by 42 feet long. The fireplace, side board, and paneling are of African mahogany, below an elaborate plaster frieze." (From Historic Galveston, by Richard Payne and Geoffrey Leavenworth, Herring Press, Houston, 1985). Interesting to note that Mr. Tyndall, the architect, ended his career as an employee at The U.S. Army Engineer's Office in Galveston. Tragically the chief mason for the house was killed during the construction when one of the stone arches collapsed.

"With all its pretension, the house ends up as the least inventive and the least beguiling of the great Galveston houses". He also called it "a grim, pedestrian, expensive pile" (From The Galveston That Was, by Howard Barnstone, Rice University Press, Houston, Published in Association with The Houston Museum of Fine Arts, 1993).

By this time only four of her six children remained. Anna Laura, the second daughter, had recurring health problems. She went away to boarding school with her sister Kate, but at age 24 was living at home. She married a Dan Moody (no relation to the Moody who purchased the mansion), and shortly thereafter died childless.

In 1888 Lee Worsham Willis, married and the father of two children," the younger scarce 24 hours old at the time of its father's death", died after a long and lingering illness.. Described as" a young man of many noble traits of character, and by his affable manner and generous disposition he made warm friends of all with whom he was thrown in personal contact. The funeral procession will move from the residence of Mr. R. S. Willis" From the Obituary in <u>The Galveston Daily News</u>, Tuesday, May 8, 1988. R. S. Willis in his will set up a trust to support the widow and the two children. Two years later Lee's widow, Fanny Denson Willis, married an English cotton broker named Worrell. This is "Aunt Fanny" who died in 1942 at her home in The Galvez Hotel in Galveston.

THE FAMILY OF
RICHARD AND NARCISSA WILLIS

Short Adam Willis

Katherine Eiza Willis
b. Galveston, 1853
M. Beverly P. Grigsby
Died Bardstown, Ky., 1932

Beatrice Olive "Betti" Willis
b. Galveston, 1871
m. Francis Walthew, 1890
Died

kate willis

olive willis walthew

Richard Martin Willis
b. Galveston, 1868
Died New Jersey, 1909

Richard willis

Short Adam, her oldest son, was no longer living at home. In March, 1894 he married Mary Carter Hawley, some 20 years younger than he (the same age as his little sister Betti) and moved out just as Narcissa was taking possession of her mansion. With a new wife and life of his own, he no longer had time or inclination to cater to his mother. Money became a major source of conflict between them as she continued to pour funds into the mansion.

Her daughter Kate went to school in Bardstown, Kentucky, met and married Mr. B. P. Grigsby raising a family of six children. Their business was "Grigsby & Co., (Incorporated), Seeds, Hardware – Farming Implements, Buggies & Wagons Bardstown, Kentucky"—seems the apple doesn't fall far from the tree. In his Will Kate's father said he had advanced to her $25,000.00 which he expected to be reimbursed to the estate out of her inheritance – perhaps this was a loan - the seed money to help the young couple get started.

Beatrice Olive Willis, was born June 15, 1872 to a 43 year old mother, a 50 year old father, with siblings who ranged in age from 23 years to five. She was indeed the baby of the family. They called her "Betti". She witnessed the death of sister Anna Laura when she was 12, and the death of brother Lee when she was 16. She met Francis Albert Walthew, whose father was a ship broker from England, and after a brief courtship they were married at Trinity Episcopal Church in Galveston on October 30, 1890. Betti was 19, Frank ten years older. Their first child, Katherine Phyllis, was born about a year later. Witnesses to that baptism were brother Short Adam and Mamie Hawley, later to be Short's wife. Betti gave birth to a son in 1893 who died within a year. In 1896 she had a second son, Gerald Francis. The family by then was living in Seabright, New Jersey.

Only her son, Richard Martin, remained to move into the new house with Narcissa.

Continuing to assert her new authority, Narcissa ultimately did three things that not only separated and alienated her children but caused the demise of the mercantile empire her husband had devoted his life to.

First, on May 2, 1894 she signed a document giving her shares of stock and controlling interest in P. J. Willis & Bro. to her youngest son, Richard M. Willis, thereby taking control of P.J. Willis & Bro. and a major source of income from Short Adam, thus alienating him forever. Richard was 26 years old, with no business experience – his only qualification was that he did not talk back to her. It proved to be disastrous for the business.

Secondly, on the 30th of September, 1897 she signed her final Will. Richard, her husband, in his Will simply gave each of the five children equal shares of his estate. Narcissa gave $50,000 to Betti Olive, 25,000 to Kate Grigsby, $10,000 to Short Adam, nothing to Richard Martin (as he had already received his inheritance in P.J. Willis & Bro. stock), a legacy to her niece, and established a trust for those grandchildren living at her death. In so doing Narcissa played favorites among her four children, an obvious cause for resentment and jealousy. To avoid the consequences of such favoritism, she further specified that anyone who objected to any portion of her Will would be disinherited.

And thirdly, to add insult to injury, on November 18, 1897 she signed a codicil to her Will giving the newly built mansion "and all that pertains thereto have and hold forever in her own right" to her youngest daughter Betti Walthew. The other three children (Short, Kate and Richard Martin) banded together to protest. Richard Martin acted as spokesperson because he (being the only one who did not inherit under the Will) had nothing to lose). He contested on the grounds that the Will was no longer the final Will and Testament, but rather the codicil. On February 16, 1900, the presiding judge ruled that the Codicil and Will were both to be honored as the final Will and Testament of Narcissa Willis.
Narcissa died September 6th, 1899 while visiting her daughter Betti in New Jersey.

Betti and Frank had no desire to return to Galveston and live in the mansion,, so they put it on the market. "Legend has it that she had a number of offers for the house, including a rather low offer of $20,000 from William L. Moody, Jr. However, on September 5, 1900, a devastating hurricane pounded the island. In its wake was destruction of lives, property and wealth." (From the archives of The Moody Mansion)
The Walthews were in the house when the storm hit. A letter written by Joseph Henry Hawley describes their experience." All the glass on the east side of the Willis' residence was blown out, and many of the beautiful wall frescoes, put in at heavy cost, were ruined. Frank Walthew made his house a place of refuge for all persons during the storm". It is said that the Walthews left Galveston immediately for the safety of New Jersey, taking with them only a few bags of their personal possessions. All offers on the house vanished with the exception of Mr. Moody. Negotiations resumed between he and the Walthews, with the result that the house was sold by the end of September for the sum of $20,000. (From Archives of the Moody Mansion) Some three years later Betti Walthew returned to Galveston and approached Mr. Moody concerning the ownership of the contents of the house i.e. the family silver, paintings, furniture etc. Mr. Moody reminded her "that she was anxious to dispose of it [the house] at his price of twenty thousand dollars, and at the time of sale she was not interested in stipulating items". The deed reads "house, grounds and all therein (deed in Galveston courthouse), and that as she was three years in getting back to Galveston to check the contents of the house, he considered the sale final, complete and for the twenty thousand dollars cash he had paid her". (As reported by Richard and Genevieve, who attribute this information to Mary Moody Northern, daughter of Will Moody).
And the house still stands. The Moody family lived in the house and on their death it became the property of their daughter, Mary Moody Northern. In 1991 she paid for the complete remodeling of the house, and opened it to the public as the Moody Mansion Museum, complete with docents and guided tours, a fitting representation of Galveston's "golden" age.

Richard Martin Willis, the youngest son, had a reputation as a party boy. In July, 1906 an item in the social column of the paper told of a house party involving Lee Willis and visiting college friends. "An uncle, Mr. R. M. Willis of New York, is also a member of this house party, and whatever the plan Mr. Willis enters into it with a will, the outcome of which is that the friends of this household are enjoying with them a informal good time and a hearty welcome by means of social feting".

A telegram sent December 29th, 1909 to Short Adam Willis states "Dick ill at 338 Park Ave East Orange. No hope Come or phone 1459 R East-Orange. Olive Walthew. Richard Martin died the next day. On January 3, 1910 a telegram to Short A. Willis reads "Uncle Dick's remains interred at eight o'clock this morning. Laura (Denson Willis)"

"Richard Martin Willis was married and divorced three times but had no issue. At the time of his death, besides his three divorced wives, one lady from France, one from New York and one from London arrived, claiming shares of his estate (information from" Aunt Fannie" Worrell) but, as there was no estate, Short Adam Willis paid for his brother's funeral"(from notes by Richard11 and Genevieve). Mr. Walter Grover, who says his children are descended from this family, wrote "Richard Martin Willis married Minnie Cassidy in 1889, there was no child, she divorced him. He married the second time Mabel Prettyman, widow Prettyman, with a three year old child, George Prettyman. She never had a Willis child, and she too divorced him. The third connection was, according to my informant, a common-law affair, without issue. When taken ill, he went to his sister, Mrs. Walthew, saying the lady had deserted him. Mrs. Walthew nursed and cared for her brother, and he died in her home. He is buried in the Episcopal cemetery in Galveston." By the time he died at age 41 he evidently had run through his inheritance, as there is a notarized statement on file dated June, 1915 as follows: C. N. Jones to The Public – The State of Texas, County of Galveston. Before me, C. Harper Anderson, a Notary Public in and for Galveston County, Texas, personally appeared C. N. Jones, known to me and who is a creditable witness, and who being first duly sworn, deposed and says that he was well acquainted with R. M. Willis, who was one of the heirs at law of Richard S. Willis, deceased, that the said Richard M. Willis died intestate on or bout Dec. 29th, 1909 in East Orange, New Jersey, and he left no estate, and that no administration proceedings were had upon his affairs and that there is now no representation of his estate in the State of Texas with authority to act for and bind his estate. Galveston, Tx., June 17th 1913.C. N. Jones

By 1909 the four Willis children were no longer living in Galveston, P. J. Willis & Bro. was basically out of business, and the only reminder of the long and productive lives of Richard and Narcissa is their grave marker "In Loving Memory" in The Trinity Episcopal Church Graveyard. But the family connection to Texas is not over. The consequences of their lives will be manifested in the next generation.

P. J. WILLIS & BRO.

Peter J. Willis.   Rich'd S. Willis.

Office of P. J. Willis & Brother,

Wholesale Dealers in General Merchandise,

Cotton,_____   *Willis' Building,*
Hides,_____
Gold,_____   Strand, Galveston, Sept 12ᵗ 1871

N. H. & J. R. Davis   Montgomery   **Folio** 490

In Account Current with **P. J. WILLIS & BROTHER.**
Willis' Buildings, Corner Strand & 24th Streets.

Galveston, Texas, July 1ˢᵗ 1877

It is Understood and Agreed that this Account is Payable at the Office of P. J. WILLIS & BROTHER, Galveston.

P. J. Willis & Brother

WILLIS BUILDING.

Office in New York,
36 Thomas St.
Office in Boston,
81 Pearl St.

Galveston,_____ 188

MONTHLY STATEMENT

Galveston, Texas, Nov 9 1895

M. Wismbush Cumberland

To *P. J. Willis & Bro*
(Incorporated)

Peter Willis once wrote "I have ever been opposed to pardnerships" and yet he went through a series of partnerships before settling on his brother Richard, a partnership that lasted 30 some years.

From the letter of February 17, 1839, written by William H. Willis from Houston, Harris County: "Peter and Mr. Hix had just bought this tract of land which we hair at work on now and rote to Richard and me to come down & go in with them which we readily agreed to and we hair all equally concerned in it". They were also in the wood business. "We are getting along very well in the wood business –we have sold during the last month $500 worth of wood".

Four months later, in a letter dated June 28, 1839, Peter wrote "We have finished paying for our tract of land and have got deed for it and that recorded. I have since bought Mr. Hicks his part being one fourth, also his part of the wood that cut and improvements for $700 and paid $200.00 cash, the balance in four months".

Peter first had a store in Houston by 1841, as proven by this ad that ran in The Telegraph, December 29th, 1841:"For sale or rent. Two small farms two miles below Houston on Buffalo Bayou with comfortable dwelling & out houses. The above property can be had on reasonable terms, for further particulars inquire at the store of the subscriber second door in the Long Row. P.J. Willess, December 25th".

(From Gone To Texas, Geneological Abstracts from The Telegraoh and Texas Register - 1835 -1841, compiled by Kevin Ladd, Heritage Books, Inc.) We can assume that this ad meant that Peter was selling out preparatory to his move to Washington-on-the-Brazos, where he opened a store. The two boys were working at nearby "Ringold Farm".

When William died, in 1843. Richard left the farm to join Peter, they moved to Montgomery, and opened the first store of their partnership. An ad in The Montgomery Patriot, July 2,1845 reads Just received and will constantly keep on hand, a general assortment of DRY GOODS and GROCERIES. P. J. Willis & Bro.

"Peter J. Willis and his brother were the opposites of each other, and formed a rare combination of unity and strength. Peter was the creative, while Richard was the executive head of the firm. These positions were assumed at the commencement of their commercial career and as the scope of their operation became enlarged and more intricate, they became more sharply defined. Peter had wonderful creative powers, great versatility and broad and well defined views of trade, knew its wants, and was energetic in supplying its demands, but as to its minute details and the management of its financial concerns this was wholly entrusted to the calm, dispassionate, and unerring judgment of his brother".

(From Galveston, History of the Island and the City, Charles W. Hayes, Vol. 2.)

"Peter James was also extremely funny and his brother Richard Short, who was extremely dignified, was heartily ashamed of him on all occasions". (From notes of Margaret Sealy Burton, granddaughter) "Both were very large, heavyset men. They showed a striking resemblance to each other. Peter James was interested in banking, factoring and merchandising. P. J. Willis, according to records, was not the visionary as was R. .S. Willis, nor was he as interested in man as an individual"

"Records show the brothers able to have been compatable, of one mind in business and of one heart in their personal relationship. However, records also show their tastes and temperaments to have differed widely especially in their selection of wives and their mode of governing their families. (From notes by Richard 11 and Genevieve)

The Montgomery store built success on credit and trust. "They kept no books in their wholesale grocery firm in Montgomery, merely chalking on the walls of the store with hunks of charcoal when an order was sent out to a customer or goods purchased from out of town. Once, when a new clerk insisted on their sending a bill to an old customer, they lost his trade forever because he was insulted for being asked to settle up, saying he had dealt for years with them and never been asked to pay until he wanted to". (From notes by Margaret Sealy Burton)

In a letter dated January 3, 1846 Peter wrote" The great failure of the cotton crop this season will brake into our arrangements very much as our collections depended principally upon cotton as it is the only thing exported out of this country. We have a good deal out and will have to waight till the people make another crop for a great portion of it. We have managed so as to keep out of debt ourselves, sold a good many goods for a good profit got but little cash on hand and is about as near as I can tell you about our business ending 1846 without giving you the particular amounts which we don't exactly know yet but will as soon as we can make a balance sheet of it".

They expanded their territory by the use of eight and ten yoke oxen teams. "I went into the office of R. S. Willis to bid him good-bye. Grasping my hand, he exclaimed "Ziegler, I wish you luck in the Bayou City that I have always loved. Be seated while I relate to you some of those incidents of the happiest days of my life, when my brother and I used to ox-team in to Houston from Montgomery County."

"I recall sitting in the office of P.J. Willis and Brother when R. S. Willis was handed a telegram from Captain M.M. Roberts, one of his star salesmen, who covered West Texas for the firm. The telegram read "Attacked by the Indians. Escaped in my ambulance with two Milburn wagons." This attack occurred near Mason, Texas in 1882. (From Tales of the Coast Country, by J. A. Ziegler)

"The firm had accumulated this cotton and held it during the critical period of the war.

They placed guards, constables and deputy marshals on duty to guard it., but there came to him a good friend to warn him that the Confederate government was about to seize the cotton and conscript it for war purposes. Mr. Willis went to the firm of Ranger & Co., operating here and the largest company of its kind in the world at that time, and stated that he wanted to sell them his cotton. Upon inquiring as to what price he wanted, he replied "If you will give me this minute on account your draft on London for 1000 pounds, you may have the lot for of 600 bales for 6 cents a pound." The draft was passed and the Rangers, being German with a London connection, as aliens neither the Confederate nor the United States government could touch them."

(From <u>Lives of the Willis Brothers</u> by J.A. Ziegler)

In 1850 Richard writes his father:" Our business continues to increase as the country does & we are getting more out & some in & on hand. So we are becoming more and more identified with the country so much so that we consider ourselves settled in this place & business for life, accidents excepted."

In April 1850 Peter wrote his parents: "we have started a business in the adjoining county and gave my brother-in-law an interest in it. C. W. Cawthorn – commenced the first of last summer – have done a fair business so far".

In a letter written from Montgomery, dated January 17th, 1854 Richard writes: "Our business & business relations with all is as good and satisfactory as we could reasonably wish – the more we doe the more we make & then we have to doe – so I could say the more a person has the more trouble they have in taking care & managing it. Our sale last year was near $50,000 out of which I think we will realize a handsome profit. At Anderson we sold $3000 worth of goods at the same time making in all about ninety three thousand dollars".

"Some time after he and his brother became established at Montgomery, they enlarged their sphere of operations and established a house at Anderson, Grimes County, taking in as a partner Mr. E. W. Cawthorn, a brother-in-law of P. J. Willis; the firm being known as Cawthorn, Willis & Bro. The business steadily increased from year to year, as the country became more densely populated, and by their thrift and economy they amassed quite a fortune.

The next move was to Houston in 1858, forming a partnership with S. McIlhenney "an old pioneer already engaged here, and the three operated under the name McIlhenny, Willis & Bro. They had the first wholesale house in Houston, dealing in groceries, dry goods, boots, shoes, etc., and rapidly became a house of great prominence and influence. Sales were made as far west as New Mexico and up into Oklahoma. They also supplied the United States government forts and commissaries extending in a chain from Brownsville north and west to Fort Sill. Okla., their commodities being delivered to these points by immense caravans of ox trains." (From <u>Lives of the Willis Brothers</u> by J.A. Ziegler.

In the period of the Civil War "the Willis brothers did not join the general exodus of the larger mercantile establishments to Matamoros, but remained in Houston and increased proportionately the volume of their business against a lessened field of competition. Meanwhile they had reorganized and now conducted the business as P. J. Willis & Bro., their associate, Mr. McIlhenney, having died during the interim". (From <u>The Lives of the Willis Brothers</u> by J. A.Ziegler)

An ad on page 4 of the Houston City Directory for 1866

P. J. WILLIS   R. S. WILLIS

          P. J. Willis & Bro.

Successor to McIlhenney, Willis & Bro.

    Main Street, HOUSTON, TEXAS

    WHOLESALE DEALERS IN

    General Merchandise

We keep on hand a full assortment of Dry Goods, tc..

Hats., Boots, Shoes and Clothing, Crockery, Hardware, Iron, Steel, Nails, Castings, &c., Groceries, Blacksmith's Tools.

"The business of the house was largely extended and expanded by the Willeses, and was quite prosperous until the War paralyzed trade. In 1867 they transferred the base of their operations from Houston to this city (Galveston), and opened out on the northwest corner of Twenty-Third and Strand Streets. In 1868 the firm purchased property on the corner of Twenty-fourth and Strand, 85 by 185 feet, and began the erection thereon of their present massive business house. This is one of the largest wholesale establishments in the South, erected at a cost of $140,000, completed and occupied in the fall of 1869".

    "Since their removal to Galveston the firm have enlarged and extended their operations until their business ramifications extend throughout the Southwest, and their trade has assumed colossal proportions." (From <u>Galveston, History of the Island and the City</u>, Charles W. Hayes, Jenkins Garrett Press, Austin, Texas 1974, Volume 2, pp 948-951.)

"As improving their position for serving the trade, Willis & Bro. now moved their business to Galveston. There they continued to expand until, in their land, they were the recognized leading wholesale house of the state. It was in the height of their career – 1882 – 1883 – that Texas produced the greatest cotton crop, acreage considered, the state has ever known. Of that tremendous crop, Willis & Bro. alone, on a factoring basis, handled 86,000 bales, a record perhaps not since equaled, and transacted a general merchandise business exceeding $11,000,000.00. (From <u>The Lives of the Willis Brothers </u>by J.A, Ziegler)

"At first they ran a modest merchandise business, but it expanded with the growth of the city. By the 1870's the firm was among the largest wholesale firms in America.

The business was on the Strand, occupying almost an entire block. Andrew Morrison, writing in 1887, speaks of two connecting brick structures – one 120 feet by 128 feet – four stories high, the other 86 feet by 120 feet, three stories high with a total floor space of over 1000,000 square feet. These buildings had steam elevators, and there was a private railroad siding at the rear of the mammoth establishment where railroad cars could be loaded with merchandise for shipment to customers throughout Texas, Louisiana and Mexico. Of all the merchandising firms operating in Galveston, this was perhaps the oldest". (From The Galveston That Was by Bernard Barnstone, Rice University Press, Houston, Published in Association with The Museum of Fine Arts, Houston, 1993.)

Peter wrote to Arthur from New York on October 20, 1868: "Richard wrote me to come home immediately as he is worked down. We are selling more goods than we ever sold before and it has kept me busy all the time buying and shipping. Used up all our money and gone in debt".

On March 31, 1871 Peter wrote Arthur from Galveston: "Business is very dull though we are selling a good many goods. Our sales last year amounted to two -2- millions ---we are collecting little or nothing out of this large amount we have out."

In addition to their merchandizing, the Willis brothers made a habit of buying land. Peter wrote to his brother Arthur in1861 evidently speaking of the coming of the railroad: "through Montgomery County, where we own a great deal of land and it is advancing very fast. I bought ten thousand acres of land when I was up there at court at an average of one dollar an acre and I do think I will make as many options dollars in a few years as there is a very large emigration setting in and will follow the line of Railroad."

In 1871 he wrote Arthur   "The Lewis suit is just decided in our favor and decreeds to us a title to 4650 acres of good land and near a RRoad now building through this country which I think in a few years will be very valuable. My headright 640 acres lies right in the center of this county and the President of the Company has promised me a Depot on it and call it Willis and the County Cite and Court house will be moved thare, which I think will make it quite a town if this turns out & I will deed a town lot to you as a present so as to make you a real estate owner in Texas. My old friends here in this country are anxious but have not fully decided the name to be Willis or Willisburg".

One of their ventures was at nature's sanitarium-old Spur Lake., located in the "Big Thicket "of east Texas. "The lake was constantly boiling and bubbling caused by gas escaping from the earth. Cures ranged from baldness to rheumatism. This property was sold in 1882 to

P.J. Willis & Bro. of Galveston, who had the capital to improve the wells and built bath houses and a luxurious two-story hotel in white-columned, deep verandah southern style.

The Springs Hotel was well managed. There was good food, companionship for those who wanted to compare ailments and the progress of cures, and at night there was dancing. Soon the resort attracted many wealthy and socially prominent people, and Sour Lake was frequently referred to as "The Saratoga of the South". (From Tales From the Big Thicket, edited by Francis E. Abernathy, University of Texas Press, Austin and London, 1966. pp. 171-189). Mr. Ziegler says the property was purchased by others at a Sheriff's sale in the "Nighties" and burned shortly after.(Interesting to note that over a hundred years later two of Richard's great granddaughters would open a spa-resort just north of Houston).

Peter died in 1873, leaving behind 5 heirs – three daughters and two sons - and appointing Richard as executor of his estate. "the manner of dividing the land was in itself unique. R.S. Willis held one-half, the remaining half to be divided equally among the five heirs. The land involved amounted to some 500,000 acres. It was ticketed according to location and value, say, one acre of rich interior agricultural land against five acres of uncultivated East Texas soil. Tom F. Laws, their land man and salaried attorney, took part in the numbering or classifying or equalizing, the farmlands. R.S. Willis always wore a "two-story" beaver hat – the remainder of his immaculate ensemble completing a picturesque appearance. On the day the estate was to be divided he called me into his office and asked that I participate in the division of the land. It was a simple drawing from his beaver hat in which had been placed 10 tickets calling for itemized properties of equal value. At his request I passed the beaver hat around and the five heirs of P.J. Willis (Peter J. Willis, William Willis. Joe Goldthwaite, and Wm. F. Ladd) drew one ticket each as representing his or her share of real estate. After they had drawn, the remaining five tickets represented one half of the estate devised to Richard S. Willis."

From (From The Lives of the Willis Brothers by J.A, Ziegler)

With Peter's death, Richard assumed full responsibility for the burden of running the huge enterprise, but had the help of Peter's oldest son, William H., who managed the Galveston branch in the home office, while Short Adam, Richard's oldest son, was living in Liverpool, England, managing the European office.

Hard times came in 1884, as related by Richard in his letter to brother Arthur dated October 17, 1884. He wrote "as to business never have I seen it so dull and depressed & I see no hope for any material improve until after another crop is made. We have had two short cotton crops in our state & it has pretty well flattened business out here we have discharged ½ of our store help & will have to reduce the salaries of the Bal – so as to bridge over – until a crop is made."

Tragedy came when, in 1888 William died in a gun accident at his home. Short Adam returned to Galveston to assist his father. He was named Comptroller, head of the firm P..J. Willis & Bro. to work with Robert Groce of Galveston as Trustee of the P.J. Willis estate.

Richard S. Willis died four years later on July 26, 1892. From 1892 – 1894 Short Adam was in control. "During his years as Comptroller Short Adam had successfully managed to keep the bulk of the Willis fortune operational. As head of the firm his life's ambition was to strengthen the business and hold its integrity."(from notes by Richard 11 and Genevieve)

"On May 2, 1894 Narcissa Worsham Willis signed an agreement giving all her shares of stock in P. J. Willis & Bro. to her youngest son, Richard M. Willis and appointing him her attorney with power to transact all business for her. Short Adam thereby lost a large portion of his inheritance and control of the company he had been running as President."
   (From notes by Richard 11 and Genevieve.)

In a letter dated May 8, 1894, written from NY City, Short wrote his mother:
   "I have received your wonderful Document in which you have robbed yourself in order to do something underhanded against Mrs. Walthew and myself for the benefit of a man who has never turned a hand for you.
   You have given Mr. R, M. Willis everything you possess, both in and out of the business for which he agrees to pay you 10,000 of your own money – for which you agree to pay him 5000 of your own money. All business connected with your estate has been and is still done in the office of P. J. Willis & Bro and costs you nothing. Being still President of this incorporation the great insult with which you attempted have stabbed me in the back. I am not likely to forget.
   If since I left home you have by chance (it will be something new) found some decent man whom you cannot bribe to boot lick you – show him that document - ask – and if he doesn't tell you that you are crazy and your childe second son a d---d rascal – then I don't know what I am talking about."

Your first son,
S. A. Willis

About a year later Short Adam resigned his position and moved with his wife and new daughter to New York, ultimately settling in Litchfield, Conn. Except for legal and estate matters he severed all relationship and communication with his mother and siblings.

It took some 11 or 12 years to settle the R.S. Willis estate – it was a very large estate, but the animosity between the heirs was certainly a contributing factor.

A letterhead for P.J. Willis & Bro dated 1905 lists T. J. Groce, President, C. H. Jones, Vice-President, G. W. Gary, Secretary – no mention of any Willis family members.

It would seem that many factors led to the unraveling of this great firm: the death of the two founding partners, Peter J. and Richard S., the death of the two first cousins (Wm. Willis, son of Peter J and Lee, son of Richard S.), the destructive decisions of the widow Narcissa, the autocratic manner of Short Adam, the ineptitude of Richard Martin. The Willis line produced few males. It was unfortunate that the males either died or were not interested or incapable of continuing in the footsteps of Peter and Richard 1.

The rise and fall of P.J.Willis & Bro. is a classic example of "from shirtsleeves to shirtsleeves in three generations".

ZACHARIAH LANDRUM
LETITIA TINES

The grandfather of Narcissa Worsham Zachariah Landrum, earns his chapter in our history our first ancestor in Texas. His story has been told and retold by people much more qualified as historians than I, thus my focus will be on how he relates to the story of our family.

Born in South Carolina in 1766, of Scottish descent, Zachariah was the third generation of his family to serve his country - his grandfather Samuel in South Carolina - his father Thomas in Virginia - and Zachariah in Georgia. At 18 years of age he received his first land in Franklin, Co., Ga. as bounty for his service. In 1795/96, at age 30, he married Letitia Tynes/Tines, ten years younger. She was the daughter of Henry Tines, a deserter of the British army (there is surely a story there). The couple later lived in Mississippi and in Alabama. He inherited 100 acres of land from his grandfather Thomas. In 1829, Zachariah and Letitia sold out in Alabama and began their trek to the state of Coahuila and Texas. They went to join the settlement of Stephan F. Austin. "Austin's first settlers, although actually only 297 land grants were made, were called the "old Three Hundred". These families were able to choose some of the best farming land in Texas. Most of these people came as farmers from the United States, but a substantial number arrived as men of means." "The vast majority emigrated to Texas for no other reason than economic opportunity; the chance to get cheap land. Some left debts behind in the states, but most brought some form of capitol: seeds, equipment, stock, or slaves." From <u>Lone Star, a History of Texas and the Texans</u>, by T. R. Fehrenbach,, Collier Books, New York.

It would seem that Zachariah fell into the "men of means" category, considering the size and composition of his caravan. In the group, in addition to Zachariah and Letitia, were two sons, William and John Landrum, with their families, one daughter, Sarah Landrum and her husband, William M. Rankin, and her family, plus Zachariah's older brother B. L. Landrum and his family. In addition they took along their slaves, and "he drove the first full-blooded Durham dark-red cattle to the eastern part of Texas". From <u>The Herald, Vol. 10 #4, Winter, 1987</u>, Montgomery County Genealogical and Historical Society. *(22)

Two months were spent on the journey. The principal land route to Texas was the road from Louisiana to San Augustine and Nacogdoches in Texas, crossing the Sabine River border at Gaines Ferry. This was not an expensive trip—some ferry fees and perhaps, wagon repairs. "Many immigrant families were practically self-sufficient enroute, for their carefully hoarded stocks of food were supplemented by game." (From <u>The Texas Republic, A Social and Economic History</u>, by William Ransom Hogan, University of Texas Press, Austin.)

Arriving January 20, 1930 they found protection from the Indians at Nacogdoches Old Stone Fort. In May Zachariah went to the Municipality of Washington town of St. Felipe d'Austin to apply for his Colonization of the Spanish Land Grant in the State of Coahuila & Texas. "The oath these colonists took has been preserved in Spanish records; it was later changed slightly to meet the circumstances of Mexican independence: "In the name of

God, Amen. A solemn oath of fidelity to our Sovereign, and to reside forever in his Royal Dominions, and to manifest this more fully, put their right hands upon the Cross of our Lord Jesus Christ, to be most faithful vassals of His Most Catholic Majesty, to act in obedience to all laws of Spain and the Indies." Family lore is that Zachariah, being a staunch Baptist, while his right hand was on the cross, held his left hand behind his back with his fingers crossed. True or not, he signed the required papers, and on April 10, 1831 received his League of Land. "In return for this oath each colonist received title to land at terms unheard of in the United States. The rich river bottoms along the Brazos...from the vicinity of Navasota... were parceled out as follows: one labor (177 acres) to each family engaged in farming; one sitio or legua (4,428 acres) to each family head who planned to raise stock. For obvious reasons – although this was plantation land and these men were Southern planters – most colonists classified themselves as stock raisers". (From <u>Lone Star A History of Texas and the Texans by T. R. Fehrenbach</u>, Collier Books, New York)

It is said that the anticipation of good land for raising cotton was as much of a lure for settlers as was the promise of free land. It was this anticipation of cotton crops that caused the inclusion of slaves in the migration. However, bringing along his stock of Durham cattle entitled him to receive the league of land. It would seem Zachariah planned this venture well.

The fact is our family had slaves is something we are certainly not proud of. It is appalling to read the Wills and realize that they parceled out slaves just as they did livestock and household goods. "Common property left by decedent between her and her husband Jeremiah Worsham the Administrater – a female slave $1000 DoDo ...2 horses $140.00 ...5 mules ...$265 a female slave aged 18 ...$250...a wagon valued at $80". (From Inventory and Appraisement of Estate of Katherine Worsham)

"The entire existence of this glittering cotton empire was based on the subordination and labor of the Negro slaves. There were 182,000 blacks in bondage in Texas, approximately one-third the entire population. The planters themselves never successfully rationalized the institution in moral terms. They recognized it as "peculiar", and justified it from the fact that it had "always" existed, and that the negro was racially inferior and could fill no other social role. The people who lived where there were no concentrations of negroes could demand emancipation on moral grounds, without really thinking through the problems of citizenship, adjustment, and social role. The whites of Texas and the south could not. Negroes, in dozens of counties, outnumbered them, rich and poor alike. To ignore ethnic attitudes and consciousness was simply to ignore or try to set aside all human history."

(From <u>Lone Star A History of Texas and the Texans</u>, Revised Edition, T. R. Fehrenbach, Collier Books, New York)

Edward Ball, A south Carolinian whose family was deeply involved in slave ownership and slave trading, has written a book "Slaves in the Family" which wrestles with the problem of guilt or blame passed down from one generation to the next. His conclusion is "A person cannot be culpable for the acts of others long dead that he or she could not have influenced." I suppose that let's us off the hook. Someone said "We should have picked our own dammed cotton" (we can all agree to that)! In our 21st century – the age of entitlements – Dr. Jack Wheeler wrote "Remember you don't have to be on a southern plantation to be a slave. If you are dependent on government entitlements you just have a different slave owner".

"These rich river bottoms were part of the Southern coastal plains, with good rainfall, accessible to the Gulf. Austin described this country as the best in the world "as good in every respect as man could wish for, land first rate, plenty of timber, fine water … beautifully rolling". The Brazos bottomland was perfectly suited to the American plantation economy. Austin could not have made a better choice"

   (From <u>Lone Star a History of Texas and the Texans</u>, T. R. Fehrenbach, Collier Books, New York.)

"Zachariah's league was located on a stream called "Bedie Creek", near Iron Mound League, surveyed for Empresario Stephen F. Austin. Their first trading post was called "Town Creek After 1837, it was called 'Ole Montgomery".

   It was almost three years later, 20 Dec., 1832, that the 3rd Landrum daughter, Elizabeth, with her husband, John May Springer, and their children arrived. They lived on a tract near Zachariah. The 2nd daughter, Katherine, with her husband Jeremiah Worsham, and their family, did not arrive until 1835" (From <u>Montgomery County History</u> 1981, Compiled and Edited by the History Book Committee of Montgomery County Genealogical Society, Inc., P.O. Box 751, Conroe, Texas 77401). Katherine is our great, great grandmother. Her daughter, Narcissa, said she remembered coming to Texas in a wagon when she was seven years old.

Zachariah and Letitia had a special relationship—he considered her a partner, obviously respecting her judgment. In his Will, dated July. 1833, he leaves all of his estate, both real and personal, to Letitia, with the exception of the division of the land, giving each of his children a portion and retaining a portion for Letitia. She is appointed Executor of his estate.

Zachariah died eight days after signing this Will." Letitia and her children marked Zachariah's grave-vault with a huge tomb approximately 4 ft. high, made of hand-made bricks molded by the slaves on their plantation." The gravesite is located on the original land grant, property now owned by his great, great, great grandson.

Letitia lived another 15 years. In 1838 she registered her cattle brand as Z/L— perhaps, as one person wrote, his initials to honor her late husband or, after 5 years of managing by herself, maybe for Zachariah/ Letitia as equal partners. She died in 1848 and is buried next to her husband. The D. A. R. placed bronze Historical Markers at each of their graves in 1965.

They had two sons, John and William and three daughters: Elizabeth m. John Springer, Sarah m. William Rankin, Katherine m. Jeremiah Worsham. It is through Katherine that we trace our heritage.

JEREMIAH WORSHAM
KATHERINE LANDRUM

Born in 1789 in North Carolina Jeremiah served two terms in the military. He first volunteered in a war against the Creek Indians, later volunteering 1814 in the war against Great Britain. In February of 1813 twenty-five year old Jeremiah married sixteen year old Katherine (sometimes spelled Catharine) Landrum in Marengo County, Alabama. They had nine children::John, Josephine, Joseph, Israel, Sarah, George, Narcissa, Elizabeth, and Letitia. Their first daughter, Sarah, died at age 3. When Katherine died only four of those children were living.

Katherine and Jeramiah were the last of the Landrum family to "GTT", coming in 1835. The last two of their children were born in Texas: Elizabeth when Katherine was 38 years old and Letitia when she was 42. When she died in 1852 Katherine was 55 years old, survived by four children; Israel, Narcissa - married to local merchant Richard S. Willis and the two youngest - minors - Elizabeth - 17 and Letitia - only 11. Katherine was buried next to her mother and father. The marker for Katherine reads " Real Daughter", which is meant to indicate that her descendancy from Zachariah and Letitia Landrum has been officially authenticated by the D. A.R. There are sunken areas on the site which could indicate other unmarked graves. In 1853, a year after Katherine's death, Jeremiah remarried and had a son by his second wife..

In 1855 Jeremiah Worsham, Administrator, filed an inventory and appraisement of her estate … her separate property, and the common property left by decedent between her and her husband. There was a court action to divide the estate, perhaps indicating that the heirs could not come to an agreement among themselves or with their father, who was the Executor. However, since there were minor children who would inherit, it could be the court action was necessary to protect their interests. Richard Willis, in his Will, set up trusts for these nieces of Narcissa, so we can probably assume that Narcissa and Richard helped to raise them. Jeremiah Worsham died in 1865 at the age of 76.

CHAPTER 5

5th Generation

SHORT ADAM WILLIS

FIRST CHILD OF RICHARD AND Narcissa, Short Adam was born in 1848, about a year after their marriage. . When he was six years old his father wrote "Short is going to school and learning fast ". He lived the first fourteen years or so in Montgomery. His family moved first to Houston, then to Galveston. By 1866 Short, then 16, was attending prep school at The Burlington Classical Institute in Burlington, New Jersey. While in Montgomery he had developed a romance with a second cousin named Nannie Gay, with whom he carried on an extended correspondence. They considered themselves engaged, writing letters vowing eternal love and eventual marriage, but time and distance worked against them.

Through these letters we have some insight into Short's school experiences. He writes frequently of his sisters Kate and Annie, in school at St. Mary's Hall nearby, and of only being allowed to see them once a week. There is some indication that his brother William was there with him. He mentions running into Uncle Peter on the street "I was going downtown when I met someone muffled up in a shawl. I did not take any notice of him until he had passed me. On looking back, I recognized him. The girls were delighted to see him." At that early date he wrote something that is significant in relation to a decision he would make some 50 years later. "If you remember in my last I told you I did not like this country at all. I didn't then, but have changed my notion since then. I had as soon be here as at home. I don't like the country nor the people, but still there is something that makes me like the place. I can't tell what it is." He also wrote ""I received a letter from Pa the other day stating that he wishes me to change my location if my health did not improve. I am happy to say that I have entirely recovered. I should be sorry to have to leave here now. The school is made up principally of Southern boys from Tennessee and Texas. Two of the Tennessee boys are going to enter college next June. I think I shall enter at the same time. If I go through the regular college course, it will be four years before I can return. I can quit sooner, but they will not give me my Sheep Skin unless I go through the prescribed courses."

By August of 1866 he is writing from Nassua Hall. Princeton. N.J. He tells of going into New York City to see his mother and the girls, "The girls are enjoying themselves finely. They know as much about the City now as I do". In January of 1867 he writes of having a glorious time in Brooklyn visiting some of his Texas friends. He speaks of his brother William's return to Texas in the spring of 67 and wonders if the Montgomery girls don't find him changed and think of him as a Yankee." By August of that year he is declaring his intention to marry her, that "I go in no lady's society here at all – neither have I any desire to." at the same time mentioning that he has to poll Greek (participating in fraternity activities) and even throws in a Latin quote "remember it's in cavica honoris – act as you think best." (that would certainly make one sound like a Yankee in Montgomery). In January of '68 he learns that she is getting married and writes a very pompous letter releasing her from their so-called engagement and delivering a sermon on her life and death, signing off "Believing that I have acted as becomes a Gentleman of Honor, I am, as I ever wish to be, your affectionate Coz, Short".

But he also mails her his photograph "to let you see how Texas air has agreed with me".

He graduates from Princeton in 1870, returns to Galveston and goes to work at his father's business. On May 4, 1871, at age 22, he married Martha Estelle Cannon, age 21. Writing on the P. J. Willis & Brother letterhead, he announces his marriage. He says "and have been for nearly a week. My experience so far leads me to believe that it is a good institution." He goes on to say "It is not necessary I think, nor expected, that I should get off a rhapsody on the many excellent qualities of my wife, sufficient to say that I am perfectly satisfied." On November 14, 1876 their son, Richard Short Willis, was born. On July 11, 1877 Martha Estelle died, followed by the death of eight month old Richard Short on August 4th, 1877. It is thought they died during an outbreak of typhoid or malaria. It was at this time that he had the tomb erected in the Episcopal cemetery, so we may assume the wife and son are buried there.

Short remained a widow for over 5 years. On January 16. 1883 he married Sally Josephine Ward, the widow Cannon (interesting to note the widow's name Cannon is the same as the first wife's family name). Sally Josephine, the new bride, was 32 years old when they married, he was 35. Some three years later on September 30, 1886, Sally died. It is believed she died in childbirth, the infant not surviving. It is thought hers is the grave just by the side of the vault Short had constructed for the first wife. By age 38 Short had been widowed twice. He remained a widow for the next eight years.

All this time he had been working for P. J. Willis & Brother, his father's business. He was sent to Europe to manage that branch of the business. "During the reign of Tsar Nicholas of Russia he lived in Moscow and enjoyed it's society. Liverpool and London had been his home for ten years, New York and its gay society off and on all of his life. In middle age he was an accomplished financier, a scholar, and a wholesome skeptic. More importantly, like his father, he was a determined man whose opinions were changed only by reasoning and whose opinions were formed with deliberation". (from notes by Richard 11 and Genevieve).

When P. J. Willis died in 1873, R. S. Willis assumed the full management of the business, and was also named executor of P. J.'s estate. P. J.'s son, William,, who had been working in the business, was killed in a gun accident at his home in 1888. Short returned home to help his father. He was appointed Comptroller of the business, and "attempted to control the spending of both families. During his years as Comptroller, Short had successfully managed to keep the bulk of the Willis fortune operational. As head of the firm his life's ambition was to strengthen the business and hold its integrity".

(from notes as written by Richard 11 and Genevieve)

In 1891 he was asked by his little sister Betti Walthew to be Godfather to her first child. Attending the baptism, acting as Godmother, was Betti's girlfriend Mamie Hawley. Soon thereafter he began courting Mamie, though she was 23 years younger than he. From his letters (which she saved), he rapidly progressed from formal requests to assist Miss Hawley in "keeping Lent", to attend a reception, to calling her Little Sunshine, then Sweetheart. She went out of town to Kerrville for several weeks and that sealed his fate. He wrote "If you have any desire to make me just a little content with my otherwise hard lot – you may manifest it by coming back to me and treating me with just a little of your consideration. I love you just the same and am as I always (almost) have been - Yours devotedly, S A W." He sent her a box of candy and wrote" If you should want to see your Goddaughter you can – only don't you dare not wait for me – I'll never forgive you if you do - You little darling, how I miss you. Honest – I am utterly incapable – so far as you are concerned – only don't be too "bossy" now that you have found it out - I break my promise to kiss you just once – Always your S A W"

Short's father died July 26th, 1892. For the next two years, 1892-1894, Short, in addition to acting as head of P.J. Willis & Bro., was acting as co-executor of his father's estate. He and Mamie were married March 28th, 1894 at Trinity Church in Galveston. They purchased their first home on Ave. H between 15th and 16th Street.

"Their marriage came at a time in his life when his family and his business were a bitter disappointment to him. She was young, enthusiastic, well bred and, even though desperately poor, a wife of whom any man would be proud. In her he was determined to regain his belief in himself and find enthusiasm in living. Because of her poverty, his mother, Narcissa, publicly rejected both his wife and him. Whereupon Short Willis set about lavishing luxury on his young bride, even though his was a conservative nature, to the extent that she was the envy of Galveston society."
(from notes by Richard 11 and Genevieve).

Two months after the marriage, Narcissa signed the agreement taking away his control of the business and thereby robbing him of his income and a large portion of his inheritance. Even worse, in the business community of Galveston he was publicly humiliated. Six days later, in a letter dated May 5th, written from New York City, he wrote to his mother" the great insult with which you attempted have stabbed me in the back I am not likely to forget".

Mamie and Olive, 6 months, Galveston, Texas

With the death of R. S. Willis there began a struggle to determine ownership and control of P. J. Willis & Brother. Katherine Willis Grigsby sold her 1,000 shares in 1892. Narcissa owned 5/8, Short Adam 1/8, Betty Walthew 1/8, Richard Martin 1/8. By 1884 Betti Olive Walthew offered to sell her shares, but her offer was refused. In counter-offer Narcissa offered to have the cash value of the stock "ascertained by arbitration, without right of appeal", conditioned on Mrs. Walthew and Short A. Willis both agreeing to sell and the notes to be for such value of the stock of each less their respective indebtedness to said corporation." If Short Adam's indebtedness included the 1,000 shares of stock his father had advanced him, then he would effectively receive nothing. There is no indication that Betti Walthew had any indebtedness, so she would be paid for her shares. When Narcissa gave her shares to Richard M. on May 2, 1884 he became the owner of 6/8 shares, or controlling interest.

"Short Adam resigned from the firm and moved his family and his holdings to New York City. After leaving Galveston, Short Adam Willis' interest in business and in his Galveston relatives came to an abrupt end. His only ambition was to live in peace and comfort with his wife and children. Money ceased to have any importance" (from notes by Richard 11 and Genevieve).

Remembering that as a student in New Jersey he wrote "I had as soon be here as at home. I don't like the country nor the people, but still there is something that makes me like the place. I can't tell what it is." He did not return to New Jersey, settling instead, with his wife and child in New York City at The Marie Antoinette Hotel at Grand Boulevard and 6th Street. Short presented himself as "a retired merchant." In December of 1896 Mamie went to visit her Aunt Alice in St. Louis and he wrote "I received your telegram from St. Louis last night about 9:30 and was glad to hear that you got that far on your journey safely. I telegraphed you tonight that "we are all well - baby doing fine" which should meet you at the house tomorrow morning. As this letter will not reach you until Monday morning I will not write again, but if anything happens will telegraph. If I wrote after this the letter would not reach you, that is if you adhere to your original programme and leave on Monday night. I am threatening to go to the opera Saturday night and if nothing turns up I will make my threat good. None of your friends have called yet – so that your absence is not generally known. I hope you will enjoy your visit. With love from myself and the kid— Your Affectionate SAW "(The kid he refers to is their daughter, Olive Elizabeth, then nineteen months old.)

Sometime before 1899 the family had moved to Litchfield, Connecticut, about 95 miles north of New York City. They rented first on North Street, later on South Street. Litchfield, at that time, was a town of about 8,000, a popular summer "resort "with many city improvements – telegraph, long distance telephone, railroad and stage with exceptional mail facilities, a club house or casino, with tennis courts, ball ground, billiard table and amusement hall; so a visitor may be as quiet as he pleases or may have all the fun he wants." (From The Connecticutt Quarterly Vol. 11, 1896) *(28)

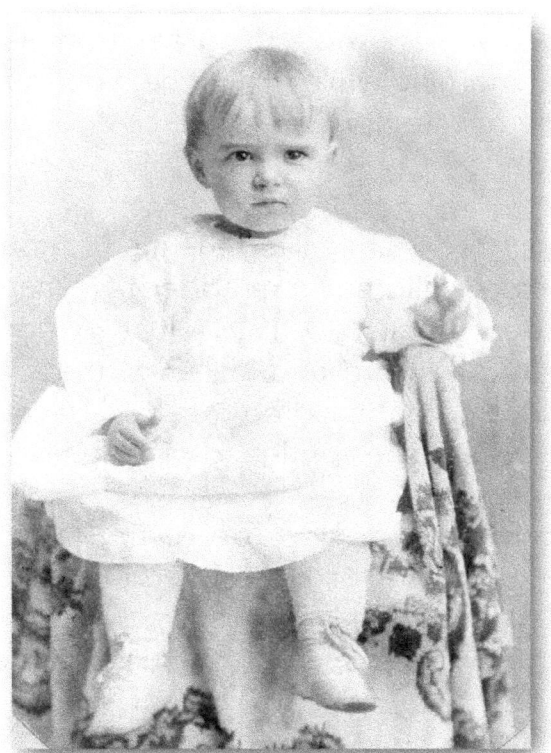

Olive Elizabeth Willis age 1

Richard Short and Henry Hawley Willis

On September 6th, 1899 Short received a telegram from his sister, Betti Walthew, telling him his mother had died that morning while visiting her youngest son Richard in New Jersey and requesting that he come or wire her.

His response is not known.

For the next eight years Short and Mamie lived the life of "country squires". Mamie stayed busy with the family – two more children were added – Richard Short, born April 20, 1902 followed by Henry Hawley, born August 10, 1903 – just 16 months apart. (although Richard and Henry are grandchildren of Richard and Narcissa, these two boys would not receive the inheritance the other eleven grandchildren received because they were born after the death of Narcissa – you mighty say she continued playing favorites from the grave).

At the second house, possibly bigger because of the addition of the two boys, there was also a barn with enough room for cows, chickens, and a horse named Texas. In September,1902 Short executed a Will giving everything to Mamie and appointing her brother, Harry Hawley, guardian of the children should both he and Mamie die before the children were of age.

Short took full advantage of his membership in The Ardsley Country Club "overlooking the Hudson River, with a private dock to accommodate the yachts of casino members, the finest and longest golf course in the world, grass tennis courts and stables on the hillside from which the stagecoach Tally Ho! Departed each weekday for the Hotel Brunswick on lower Fifth Ave". In the city he enjoyed his membership in The Princeton Club of New York, which, in addition to overnight accommodations and dining facilities, had a 10,000volume library, a squash court and a fitness center.

Mamie took the children in May, 1907 to Asbury Park, New Jersey to recover from the Whooping Cough (Olive would have been 12, Richard 5, Henry 4). On May 7th he addresses her as Mother and "notes with pleasure the fine condition and continued improvement of the kids. Hope you will take it easy and soon be well and strong – Love to all – Your Affectionate husband S A Willis." On May 10th he writes "Have your letter reciting your spree in New York. You are so well satisfied with yourself and your daughter and the good time you are having – that I won't begin to yap about how much I miss you – just let you imagine what a state I am in after two weeks absence. My appetite is all right and my "Standing Riggin" is all right, so that I manage to get along by not "thinking" too much. I play golf every day and am tired enough at night to be comfortable. You stay just as long as you wish and don't worry – Don't hunt for trouble. I kiss you good bye - Always - - your affectionate husband - S A Willis." The very next day, May 11th, he writes "Sweetheart - I am continuing to be homesick for you. Hope you were able to find something that suited in way of servants so that we can be together for a while. You have been away so much that it will be like getting "married" over again when you settle down. I kiss with much love Yr. affectionately SAW." (Short was 59, Mamie 36 – they obviously had a very close, and caring relationship—time for her to come home!).

During this time Short was in touch periodically with Galveston on matters of business. In December of 1899 he wrote to George C. Mann, his co-executor of his father's estate, asking that he (Short Adam) be paid $10,000 as a fee for his services rendered as co-executor. Mr. Mann wrote back an "I told you so" letter, saying "You will recollect that I thought you ought to charge the estate, but you refused to do so, and as to whether your refusal estops you from now charging I am not prepared to say; at present there is not half that amount on hand---and all that is likely to be needed for expenses that have been incurred…if there is ever any money on hand I will see that you have a full opportunity to get your pay before it is paid out".

To add insult to injury, Mr. Mann had signed a receipt which read "Received from the Estate of R. S. Willis, through P. J. Willis & Bro. the sum of Ten Thousand Dollars ($10,000) in full of all services rendered to date and to be thereafter rendered by us in all matters relating to the adjustment and settlement of said estate." Then when the estate was sued over a land matter, Mr. Mann graciously offers to "to represent the Estate at a fee of $250.00 in advance and $250 more on a decree being entered in the District Court. If either side appeals then such further fee as may be agreed on." Easy to see why Short lost faith in Mr. Mann. He referred to him in one letter as "that Episcopal carpet bagger". His brother-in-law, Mr. Grigsby wrote" It is true Judge Mann's receipt for Compensation as excr. would seem to cover all expenses, but it seems from the number of attorneys employed by the excrs. and Trustees of the estate of Mrs. Willis that excrs. or Trustees in Texas are not expected to attend to any legal or in fact any other business than draw the fee paid".

The other person they were dealing with was a Mr. Alvey of Texas Guarantee & Trust Company, who was handling the estate of Narcissa. Evidently Short wrote him a "caustic and totally unwarranted letter" demanding information on the estate. Mr. Grigsby called Mr. Alvey pigheaded, and said he had repeatedly asked for "a statement of the expenses of the estate, in other words what amount of money came into their hands and to whom and for what it was paid out. He did give me a gross statement of the money coming into his hands and what was left, but has refused to at any time in the past seven or eight years give me a statement of amounts paid out and to whom." Mr. Alvey's reply to Short's letter "you have not even kept the Company advised of your location and have never written a line since the death of your mother. In all my life I have never encountered as much ill humor, disrespect and thanklessness as in every member of your family with whom it has been my ill fortune to have to deal since the death of your father and mother, and until now you have been silent. The amounts I now send you have been to your credit since the respective distribution and I know of no duty I owed you to hunt you up and find out whether you wished the money or not. You knew the location of the company and if addressed respectfully would have always given you fully the status of matters". (That is not what Mr. Grigsby, who was in frequent communication, says.) Short wrote across the bottom of this letter, underlined, "This Is A Lie".

At the same time he was dealing with his younger brother Richard over the disposition of the steamboat Cumberland and of mining interests in Colorado, for which Richard is demanding a 10% commission. He is paying taxes on properties all over Texas and paying the funeral expenses for a Mr. Ward who died "with five cents in his pocket and would have been buried in the Potter's field"…Short sent the funeral home a check for $62.00… he "was given a decent burial and his grave is properly marked, if at any time you wish to know where it is".

In December, 1907 he made arrangements for the family and nurse to stay at the Hotel Gordon - 16th – Eye Streets, Northwest in Washington, D. C. – 4 private rooms and bath, board on the American plan @ $360 a month. Later they settled at 1814 Nineteenth Street. Short continued his golf and socializing through his membership in The Princeton Club and The Metropolitan Club of the City of New York, "one of Washington's oldest and most valued private institutions with a primary goal of furthering literary, mutual improvement, and social purposes. Its location and dedication to a tradition of social civility provide members with a haven from the bustle of Washington professional life, while offering amenities associated with contemporary urban life. Its proximity to the White House made it a destination for many local, national and international leaders". (It would seem that he continued to live the high life, in spite of his financial concerns. It is said that he regularly played golf in a foursome with President Taft, received invitations to social events at the White House, to have a glass of eggnog with Chief Justice Shepard, and invited to call on The President of Princeton University from a "country squire" he had become an "urban sophisticate", all the while postponing the inevitable reality…his money was running out!

Mamie who was pursuing her interest in genealogy, became very active in the D.A.R. Olive was now 14, the boys 7 and 6.

Through correspondence Short began to take more interest in the Texas holdings, using his father-in-law Col. J. H. Hawley, among others, as his agent. His increasing effort was to sell for cash—using terms like "just waiting for something to turn up…I am just holding for a higher price…I thought I would always keep this (ten acres at Alvin) as a harbor of refuge in case I "blew up" at any time. It don't take long sometimes to loose all your doe – especially when somebody else is doing the loosing – I am not going into any farm promoting scheme - I want to sell my land for cash + have it over - when I do sell. Hoping something in way of Gas, Oil, or other millionair-making jinks will happen to my land soon. If you should happen to be in Lampasas please take a look at my 9 acres of land & see what you think of its' future – How would it be as a home for my family?"

He continued to do battle with Mr. Mann, who began one letter saying "Your screed of 8th just received. If you will take an Eli Liver pill, it may assist you in writing a decent letter."

In October, 1909 he received from Mr. Alvey of Texas Guarantee and Trust Co. the final disposition of the assets due the 11 grandchildren of Narcissa Willis, in the amount of $10,900.98 cents each plus $775.89 interest, plus $360.00 per year from a note, and 3400 acres in Grimes County to be divided when sold (This was the inheritance of his daughter, Olive Elizabeth).

"In 1915 Williston was completed. Mr. Willis arrived with four boxcars of household furnishings, the Washington staff of servants and a skeptical heart. He was quite ill with diabetes and most reluctant to leave his clubs, his golf game and his interesting friends in Washington, D. C. for "the dull stultifying life of a country squire in an illiterate community in the backwoods".(from notes by Richard 11 and Genevieve) His grandchildren report that in those last years he was confined to a wheelchair with a nurse in constant attendance. There was no elevator in the house, but the Master Suite on the second floor consisted of a bedroom, a bath and dressing room, with a porch that ran all the way across the front of the house with a magnificent view, and a beautiful, huge oak tree to one side, so he could be very comfortable in his "suite". The front stairs were wide and in two sections with generous railings, so he possibly could have maneuvered those.

Short wrote his second Will on the tenth day of January, 1916. Mary Carter Willis was left everything he possessed---a modest estate –and made sole executrix. He left nothing to Olive, saying "I make no provisions for my daughter, Olive Willis Martin, for the reason that I have heretofore before her marriage liberally provided for her." He died September 27th, 1917, at age 69.

An inventory of his estate, filed December 22, 1917 lists:

1800 acres in Young County, TX	$20,000.00
10 acres in Lampasas County, TX	500.00
100 acres in Lee County, TX	500.00
Undivided ½ interest. in	
540 acres in Jack County. TX	700.00
4 lots in Liberty County, TX	150.00
220 acres in Henderson County, TX	1,200.00
200 acres in Newton County, TX	900.00
18 lots & 3 blocks in Ballinger, TX	1,000.00
Total Value	$25,550.00
Notes and accounts due	288.00
Grand Total	$26,963.00

(This is the equivalent to roughly $300,000.00 in 2015).

The marriage of Olive came as a shock and bitter disappointment to her parents. In May of 1917 she gave birth to her first child, a girl, and named her Narcissa Willis Martin. In view of his estrangement from his mother and the bitterness and resentment he felt toward her, he must have felt this was another "stab in the back".

Short Adam Willis is buried in the Episcopal Cemetery in Galveston in the large vault he had erected in 1876. He had three wives. The first wife and child are possibly buried with him. The second wife is buried just beside the tomb. Mamie intended to be buried beside him – indeed had money set aside for this specific purpose which she spells out in each of her many Wills - instead is buried in Houston. Why this happened is not clear—perhaps that money was needed to cover other expenses. One explanation is found in her Will, written August 28, 1952 in which she states "The Tomb was built long ago about 1876 and has narrow receptacles so that the modern coffins are far too large. Levy in Galveston understands this condition and must be consulted for ways of meeting the limits." Maybe Mr. Levy's solution was prohibitively expensive—in days before cremation was acceptable maybe that was not an option—whatever the reason, Mamie is not lying where she wanted to be---by Short's side.

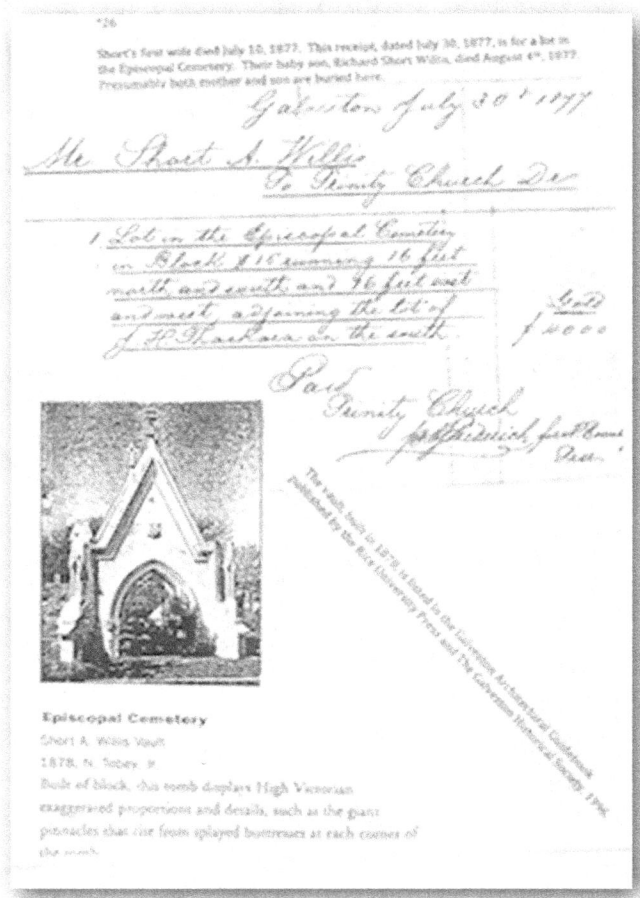

Short Adam Willis began his life's journey in Montgomery and it ended there. His was a series of far-flung adventures - more than his share of sadness and disappointments - a vast network of successful social relationships through his clubs and golf games - tempestuous business relationships caused no doubt by the imperial attitude expressed in his correspondence— a persistent self-indulgence and financial irresponsibility - a refusal to face reality and a recurring habit of simply removing himself from the scene when there was conflict. Could all this be traced back to and blamed on an unstable mother and a workaholic father?

In all fairness to him we must remember his father, who was the astute business head of P.J. Willis & Brother, was the one who appointed him comptroller of the business, he had been living abroad for a number of years and was brought home to face a family of brothers and sisters whom he barely knew and cousins on the P.J. Willis side who by now were grown and had their own ideas of how the business should be conducted. We have to wonder how differently things might have turned out had his younger brother Lee and/or his cousin Will lived – would their influence have been strong enough to control Narcissa and support Short in dealing with the family? Whatever the legacy of his life might be, his most enduring achievement was his marriage to Mamie - for all their shortcomings they were devoted to each other throughout their marriage.

> Young Short Adam, when he was a student at prep school, sent this poem to his cousin Nannie Gay:
> "Will you ever weep when I have passed away?
> When cold in death I sleep, through many a weary day?
> Will you place a wreath upon my little mound In evening's holy hour when shadows hover round?
> Will you often come to view my lowly head?
> Will you plant a flower to blossom o'er my head?"
> Mamie's answer would certainly be yes.

MARY CARTER HAWLEY

Born December 31, 1871, called "Mamie" by the family, she was the older sister to Harry. Her mother was "sensitive" and ambitious, her father loquacious and distinguished. Her family had a history of wealth and privilege. Her southern mother instilled in her a sense of entitlement and a deep resentment of the injustices of life.

At age 23 she married Short Adam Willis and began a life of luxury. Three children were born to her – first, daughter Olive Elizabeth, about a year after her marriage, then, after a gap of some seven years, two sons in rapid succession, Richard and Henry. She was an efficient mother, using the help of maids, nurses and nannies, overseeing their needs, not hesitating to ship them off at an early age to various schools and camps. She continued to pursue her own interests, mainly an obsession with genealogy, kept up voluminous correspondence with family and relatives, frequently taking breaks from domestic life to visit with various kin, go to cooler climes to rest, or shopping trips to the big city. She was a devoted wife, with a warm, loving relationship with her husband.

Mamie and Olive, age one, New York City

As a new bride and mother Mamie bravely followed her husband as they pulled up roots and moved to New York. She adjusted to life in a hotel, and then established their home in Litchfield. She maintained close ties with her mother and father in Galveston, her mother coming to stay for long visits. She went to see her Aunt Julia in St. Louis and they made a trip to Cuba to visit uncle Bradley Hawley on his sugar plantation. They received visits from Uncle Bradley in Litchfield.. Through her mother she claimed membership in The United Daughters of the Confederacy and the Daughters of the American Revolution. Other groups she joined were The Litchfield Scientific Association, The Washington Club, and The Society of Virginia Women in New York.

In 1910 she supervised the move from Litchfield to Washington. D.C., staying first at The Gordan, a residential hotel, then moving into a 5 bedroom, 61/2 bath town home in the historic area of Northwest Washington, just above Dupont Circle. (The house is still there – you can visually tour it by typing in the address – it has been completely remodeled and modernized with an estimated value today of over 2 ½ million.)

From 1910 to 1911 she served as Librarian General to the D. A. R. library, where "she rendered outstanding service in the directing and copying of manuscripts comprising 3,000 pages of Court Orders and other valuable records. She insisted on the installation of steel shelves in the library, which have proved very valuable." (From <u>Tribute</u> given at the Memorial Service D. C. D.A. R. State Conference, March 9, 1958.)

1913 was the year for Olive's debut, which Mamie planned and executed. In correspondence from cousin Alice M. Meredith of Philadelphia, dated November 29, 1910, the matter of raising daughters was discussed. After mentioning family members who had problems with their daughters, Alice writes "My, how you do have to watch girls now-a-days. Mine certainly keeps me in the jump and I don't feel like letting her out of my sight for a minute. Yes, this is her coming out – she is eighteen years and nine months old and I am unable to keep her in another year."

The "coming out" is the debut – usually done at age 18 – which is the official announcement to society that your daughter is available for marriage. Through a series of parties and the grand debutant ball the daughters are introduced to young bachelors of acceptable families in the hope that romance and a suitable marriage will follow. Olive was "on the market", and Mamie was the "huckster." For that, they needed to return to Galveston and use the connections to the Willis and Hawley relatives there. This was humbling for Mamie, but she was determined. How Olive felt about this we can only guess.

"Olive had her formal "coming out" party in Washington, D.C. - A garden party on the White House grounds, given in her honor by President and Mrs. Taft." (from notes by Richard 11 and Genevieve)

May 3. 1913 - Olive is 18 - the age for her debut

The President and Mrs. Taft

request the pleasure of the company of

Miss Willis

at a reception to be held at

The White House

Tuesday evening, January the fourteenth

nineteen hundred and thirteen

at half after nine o'clock

"Mrs. Willis, feeling that Galveston was the social center of the Montgomery area and the city from which her daughter's future husband would come, decided Olive should be presented at a formal evening reception at the Galvez Hotel. There followed a season of gay social activity for both Olive and Mrs. Willis" (from notes by Richard 11 and Genevieve.)

Short refused to have any part of it, he and the boys staying in Washington. Mamie and Olive went to Galveston, staying with her father. The local newspaper, <u>The Galveston Daily News</u>, reported the festivities: "The seventy-fourth anniversary ball given last evening by the Galveston Artillery Company at Hotel Galvez was one of the most brilliant affairs ever given at this handsome hostelry. This event opened the formal social season of 1913-14. The grand march was led by the President of the club, Mr. George Sealy, with his cousin, Miss Olive Willis, daughter of Mr. and Mrs. Short Adam Willis of Washington, D.C. and granddaughter of Col. J. H. Hawley of Galveston and of the late R. S. Willis of this city, opened the ball. Miss Willis looked beautiful gowned in caramacross (Irish) lace with hoop skirt wired with French rosebuds over white crepe meteor. She carried American Beauty roses."

"Miss Olive Willis has been feted and feted ever since her debut this season, but never has she had a more beautiful setting to foil her brunette beauty than when, Thursday afternoon, she stood beside her hostess, Miss Alice Sweeney, in the gold drawing room of the sumptuous home of the fair hostess's aunt, Mrs, Rebecca Ashton Brown, and received her friends' congratulatory "How do you do?" in a happy, graceful manner. Miss Willis wore an exquisite creation of heaven-blue charmeuse (satin, soft, moves like water)—elaborated with silk pannears and rhinestone trimmings, and a corsage of Pink Killarney roses." "Mrs. Willis and Miss Willis will entertain their friends at The Hotel Galvez December 23 with a reception and tea. The hours are 4-6 in the afternoon and 5-7 in the evening." "Miss Olive Willis returned Wednesday from a two days' stay in Houston, the guest of Miss Dorothy Robins. Miss Willis reports that the functions and the dance Wednesday night were quite pleasing events".

Their picture on the society page of that same paper with the heading "CHARMING MATRON AND DEBUTANTE DAUGHTER HAVE SPENT TWO MONTHS IN GALVESTON". The story reads "Mrs. Short Adam Willis and Miss Olive Willis of Washington, D.C. who have been in Galveston the past two months, left for a short visit Saturday to several Texas towns. On returning they will take a steamer for New York about the 15th of the month. Then they will go to their home in Washington. Miss Willis came to Galveston to make her debut, as her parents were born here. Mother and daughter have been the recipients of a number of affairs in their honor, and it is with keen regret the social world will bid them good-by."

In 1914 the decision was made to move to Texas. Age and illness had forced Short to face his mortality, and he had begun looking around for a place to retire. Pride and resentment made Galveston out of the question. He wrote "I thought I would always keep this (ten acres at Alvin) as a harbor of refuge in case I "blew up" at any time " "If you should happen to be in Lampasas please take a look at my 9 acres of land & see what you think of its' future – How would it be as a home for my family?" He was also forced to face the fact that the money was running out. He wrote "It don't take long sometimes to loose all your doe – especially when somebody else is doing the loosing."

Short turned everything over to Mamie. She hired the architect to draw up the plans, she made the necessary legal moves to obtain clear title to the property, she made arrangements for the family, supervised the construction. Short stayed in Washington until the house was ready and the family could move in, sometime in. early 1915.

The next three years were busy ones for Mamie. Getting the family moved, establishing the household and hiring the necessary help, organizing and setting up the farm required time and organization. Meanwhile she had a sick and disgruntled husband to look after and a daughter who was not happy at this dramatic change in her life. There was the nurse to help with Short. The boys were around most of the time, probably finishing the school term in Galveston and then joining the family for the summer.

Mamie was 43 years old and, for all her capabilities, she could not control everything. Who would have thought that Olive, who had been in Montgomery during the long construction process, loved horses, and spent many hours a day riding the property, would come in one day in August of 1915 to announce her marriage to a local nobody, and reveal her pregnancy, a crushing blow - the end of all Mamie's hopes and dreams for her future. Reacting in her dramatic, authoritative manner, she ordered Olive out of the house. Olive lost that baby. The two boys were forbidden to have any contact with Olive.

Short wrote out his Will in January of 1916. In May of 1917 came the birth of their first grandchild, a girl, Narcissa Willis Martin, named after the woman who betrayed them. Mamie, at age 46, became the widow Willis that September with Short's death. Now she faced life alone in this isolated world she had created, alienated from her daughter, with the daunting challenge of raising two teen-aged boys.

Montgomery was very isolated from the world., with a predominately black population. After Short's death Richard and Henry were shipped off to Stanton Military Academy in Virginia. At first Mamie's family would come to visit, but with time those visits became less frequent and her letters more pleading. Father wrote from Houston mentioning "that great big house". (Everyone, the help, the locals, etc., commonly referred to it as "the big house".) As her financial situation became more obvious, Mamie dismissed Miss Nash (the governess) and most of the servants. She lived alone, doing all of the domestic work and employing field hands for the heavy labor. At one time she even taught school at a little schoolhouse on Spring Branch Road. She entered into community affairs. One woman who had lived back up in the woods told me Mrs. Willis went before the school board and insisted they provides bus transportation for all the children in the districts, regardless of where and how far away they lived. She had a lasting friendship with one of the local teachers and with several locals who shared her interest in genealogy.

She became an excellent shot. "Before dawn one morning she was awakened by someone climbing the rose trellis outside her second-story bedroom window. She was alone in the house, as usual, with the nearest field hand asleep in the quarters over three hundred yards from the main house. She quietly waited until she heard hands grip her windowsill, then she fired the pistol which she kept by her bedside, into the darkness toward the sound. A body dropped to the ground, then she heard running feet. She got up, dressed, and, pistol in hand, went out into the night to awaken the negro foreman. After searching a bit, they found a wounded white man, dressed in prison clothes, crawling in the bushes. Mamie notified the State prison in Huntsville, and she and the negro foreman held the escapee until the prison uardens arrived." (from notes by Richard 11 and Genevieve)

"There was to be a lynching in Conroe on the courthouse square of a young male negro from Montgomery. Because of the consequences of such savagery, the leaders of the act went from house to house in Montgomery demanding, under threat, that all males over 12 years of age be present in Conroe to throw a lighted match on the pyre, thus sharing the responsibility. Henry and Richard, then thirteen and fifteen, were home from school on vacation. Mamie, though overcome with horror and disgust, listened to the civilian request with no show of emotion. She stated that her sons were visiting relatives in Galveston and probably would stay for several weeks. Upon the men's departure, she prepared to leave with the two boys. She adroitly planned to drive through Conroe (there was no other route to Houston then) after the mob had gathered but before the violence began. She put the boys on the floor in the back of her "Jack Rabbit Apperson" automobile, piled feed sacks high on the seat and then on them and drove from home in Montgomery through Conroe. On the outskirts of Conroe, going in the Houston direction., her car was stopped by an unknown white man who asked her destination, but did not search her car. This was a most fortunate circumstance for she certainly would have killed him had he tried to search." (from notes by Richard 11 and Genevieve). (This was probably related to the burning of Joe Winters, which took place in May, 1922, as related in the book White Lies by Nick Davis.) *

There is no evidence that her relationship with Olive improved, and she carried on a continuous war with son-in-law Stump, frequently communicating with him through lawyers. Early on she had a fence dispute with him, served him with a Notice and Demand, which was drawn up by an Attorney and posted in the post office in the town of Montgomery. Things went downhill from there!

On June 16th, 1917 Short Adam and Mamie borrowed $1,000.00 for one year, pledging a part of their land. The note was paid off with a cashier's check – most probably money from the sale of another property.

In September of 1918 she applied for and received a loan from The Federal Land Bank in Houston. This was a program set up by the Federal Government to loan money at low interest rate to land owners. It was the beginning of the end. By 1927, after ten years of struggling, Mamie left Montgomery, and by 1930 Williston Farms was no longer hers.

Mamie first settled in Houston. Through her activities in The League of Women Voters she became involved with Florence M. Sterling, a fellow female spirit, and went to work for her "A Woman's Viewpoint" magazine. When it folded, she went to New York. By 1930 she and Henry were living at The Madison Square Hotel. She worked as a Companion to various members of The Young Women's Christian Association.

Both of the boys married and had families-(Richard 11 to Genevieve Murphy in 1925 with three children, Henry to Marian Brock, in 1932 with one son.) Henry settled in New York. Richard moved from El Paso to Houston, to Galveston. Mamie would live with each off and on.. Marion wrote "She would receive a little money from somewhere or other and she would be off to Texas for a short time – then we would receive devastating letters and we would bring her back to New York to be with us again. She seemed to be happy with us – made friends in the neighborhood – had her friends in New York – did volunteer work at the YWCA (made beautiful dolls for their sale – worked on her family tree – going into N.Y. to the library." All the while complaining: "Neither of my sons was ever interested in my estate, never paid any taxes or agents or helped me to manage or struggle with loans or my own living expenses. So from their early marriages I made my own way."

In 1934, when Olive died, she returned to Montgomery and tried to take charge of the household and supervise the children. Her idea was to impose order on chaos – she introduced afternoon naps and no between meal snacks (there is a story of a big "brouhaha" over "who stole the Graham Crackers"). Needless to say, this was not well received by the Martin kids, who were raised by the help and accustomed to little or no discipline. Added to the rancor that existed between she and Stump, the situation was impossible and her stay was brief. Before she left Mamie proposed that she take the three youngest girls to New York to raise them. Stump's answer, putting his arms around his three youngest children, was "You will not have my girls".

In 1936 she stayed for three months in a mountain cabin in New Mexico with the three children of Richard and Genevieve while the parents sought work in Houston and Galveston.

There ensued letters of advice and admonition – evidently a trying time for all concerned. Mamie returned to New York.

By 1946 Henry had taken a job with Caltex Oil Company and moved first to Calcutta, India, then to Japan, then to the Philippines. Richard, who was on active duty with the Air Force, was in Japan. In 1948 Mamie developed severe arthritis. She had her doctor write to her sons explaining that she was no longer able to navigate living at The George Washington Hotel. She was 77 years old.

By 1951 she is at The Sheltering Arms home, an establishment run by The Episcopal Church for needy women. She wrote "in a somewhat precarious situation, assured of a Haven and receiving every courtesy and comfort but not with a pension or income like those enjoyed by the other "Ladies" accepted by Sheltering Arms. This militates against any feeling of security or entitlement."

She remained bright, alert, and interested in the world around her. She wrote to her friend in Montgomery, and wrote letters to the editor, scolding Mr. Ziegler when he wrote about Richard S. Willis 1and she did not agree with his facts or descriptions.

She wrote and rewrote her Will several times. In the one dated 1952 she enumerates the number of times she had given money to one or the other of the boys, concluding "it has been a long and sad widowhood, through which I have prayed daily to be a good mother and a help to my sons". "So I think I have done my full duty by them", closing with "Written 4 o'clock all by myself."

Mamie (Mary Carter Hawley Willis) died December 16, 1956 at the age of 84. "At the time of her death…her eyes were bright and her heavy brown hair untouched by gray." (from notes by Richard 11 and Genevieve).

Mamie had many admirable traits. Her superior intelligence is obvious. She was very much a "do'er" at a time when women were expected to stay barefoot and pregnant. She had unlimited self-confidence. She never hesitated to tackle whatever task was at hand, nor doubt her ability to do it. She was creative, sewing dresses, making dolls, etc. She was persistent, as shown by her perpetual pursuit of genealogy. She was brave and courageous, as proven in those years she lived at Williston Farms by herself. She did not admit defeat easily or graciously.

Her weakness was in the area of personal relationships. Although her father, husband and brother remained devoted to her, she had a great deal of difficulty with those outside the family (which included her children's spouses), and a rocky relationship with her three children. Olive, her precious first-born on whom she doted as a child, dramatically revolted against her and the lifestyle she endorsed. The two boys, raised as pampered princes, having to face the harsh reality of supporting a family in depression times, tried gallantly to remain loyal and supportive to her, an impossible task in the face of her criticisms and manipulations.

The poet KHALIL GIBRON wrote "Your children are not your children---you may give them your love but not your thoughts for they have their own thoughts---you may strive to be like them, but seek not to make them like you for life goes not backward nor tarries with yesterday"
     From "ON THE CHILDREN ' by Khalil Gibran.

We must acknowledge our indebtedness to Mamie, for in her own words "to each is due his or her word of respect and tenderness from us".

Mary Carter Hawley Willis

Mary Carter Hawley Age 10
The family's pet name for her was Mamie.

JOSEPH HENRY HAWLEY
SUSAN CARTER BROWN

Born in 1846 in Memphis, Tennessee, he came from a long and distinguished line, which Mamie traced back to the 1600's and England. Her notes on the family include such interesting stories as "Grandfather Hawley lost his life by reason of a fall from his horse when crossing over a bridge that had been weakened by storms. The bridge gave way and on falling Grandfather sustained injuries, which resulted in his death. Grandmother never recovered from the shock and died of what was then called "a decline". Mary Ann Carter (from whom Mamie inherited the name Carter) died of "a cold contracted at a White House ball when she was only nineteen".

Joseph Henry was born into a family of four children, he being the oldest. There followed Robert Bradley, born in 1850, Lucy Melinda, 1854, and Frank Lafayette, 1857.

"He was a very large man (over six feet four) with a large head covered with thick, snow white wavy hair and a white mustache. His eyes were large and green. Mr. Hawley was a Greek scholar, spoke French and Spanish fluently, and had an unusual command of the English language." (from notes by Richard 11 and Genevieve).

He was a graduate of the Naval Academy in the 1860's, taking training on "Old Ironsides", the ship that was launched in 1747 by President John Adams, fought in the War of 1812, and was eventually moved back to Annapolis o deploy with midshipmen for their summer training cruise.

On May 5, 1866 young Joseph wrote to his mother: Did I ever give you an account of how I live here on board "ship" – well -

All the midshipmen sleep in hammocks and have to go to bed at 9 o'clock every night and are made to rise at 6 o'clock in the morning and are allowed 20 minutes to wash dress and appear at "Inspection" which takes place every morning 61/2 A.M. and if your clothes are properly brushed or your clothes are out of order the least bit you are reported for being "untidily dressed at Morning Inspection" and I have never been reported yet for such a thing.

The class had "Fleet sailing" today and enjoyed it very much indeed as the wind was fair. Every Saturday the Midshipmen are allowed a number of boats and those who wish can go sailing. I go every Saturday. I never request a boat but am always invited to go by some of the parties going.

In a class of 126 members I am no. 5 in drawing and draughting and I am in Seamanship 16 in the first. I am only four below No. 1 and 15 from No. 1 in the Second, so you see I stand tolerably well.

It is getting very late and as it is very near 9 bells I will dash and write again on Sunday. Love to all my brothers and to my dear little sister Lucie Jean, little darling Your affectionate

Son, Henry (He signed his name Henry in his early years, but later dropped it to be known as Joseph)

At age 23, he married Susan Carter Brown. Family letters testify to her exceptional qualities of mind and heart. "She was a lovely girl with a sweet voice and a gentle disposition".

He decided not to pursue a military career. He was a great admirer of Abraham Lincoln, was in Washington when Lincoln was assassinated and it affected him deeply.

Although a true southerner by birth and tradition, he became a Republican, saying it was the party following Thomas Jefferson's principals. His day job was as traffic manager for the IGN Railroad, for which he received a modest salary, to the dismay of his wife. "He was tremendously interested in transportation and was convinced that Texas must have an excellent road plan if it were to expand industrially. Therefore, he devoted himself to lobbying for new and better roads throughout Texas, and was instrumental in obtaining bills passed to this effect. "In speeches to such towns as Cuero he urged local farmers and tax payers to vote money for a road system comparable to the one in France, to keep control local, thus avoiding the fraud and corruption that comes with the acceptance of national funds.

In 1908 he was" forced out" of the railroad position and joined a steamship agency, waxing poetic about the possibilities—"the future swells with its importance" – Galveston cannot get out of the way of the great volume of traffic which will come tumbling down with resistless force seeking the sea through this gateway." (As we know the traffic passed Galveston by, going to Houston instead by way of the ship channel)

At age 62 he wrote Mamie " "Is it not fine that I keep my health. I am thankful. It enables one to work and go forward with energy. Remember Walt Whitman's "Keep a goin." You won't get rusty if you do."

Meanwhile brother Robert Barclay was a successful businessman elected in 1896 to Congress and successfully re-elected in 1898—he was the only Republican elected from Texas. In 1906 he became President of the Cuban American Sugar Company. He and his wife were divorced. His only daughter died at age 29, leaving two small boys. He spent Christmas of 1906 with Mamie and Short in Litchfield, and visited with them when he was in Washington on business. Mamie and Olive made a trip to visit him in Cuba.

Susan Ann Brown Hawley, Joseph's wife, was a victim of her southern past. In addition to losing beloved family members in the Civil war, she evidently went through many hardships during the period of reconstruction.. Mamie wrote of her Mother" during her girlhood she saw many stirring scenes – three times was forced, with her mother and the younger children, together with four slaves who remained faithful, to vacate the houses they successively occupied. Grandmother each time was treated with courtesy and permitted to take with her such articles as she could carry, but with several little children that could not be a great deal. Her impressions of horror remained with my Mother always. She could not look at a burning house or pictures of battles without great emotion." It was through her mother that Mamie was entitled to membership in The United Daughter's of the Confederacy.

In 1908 Olive, thirteen year old, came to Galveston to spend time with her grandparents. Father wrote to Mamie" Your Mother is beaming with the simple presence of the child and the sunshine is just streaming so that all are in glee over the special holiday her visit gives us. Do you sit down quietly and look out over the space and see us three telling everything of interest to each other – our likes, our preferences, what will be agreeable and then doing them all in order with due care for health and safety of life and limb. Your Mother has made her room look like a bower for the youngster. Your Mother will stand the child's visit finely— you must relieve your mind of any anxiety—the coming of dear Olive has contributed to make her the happiest of women".

Joseph was a prolific letter writer. The two outstanding events in his lifetime were the hurricane that hit Galveston in 1900 and The Republican National Convention in Chicago in 1912. His vivid description of these make you feel you are there, his reports authenticated by other sources.

On Saturday, September 8, 1900 a hurricane swept in from the Gulf of Mexico, the center passing about thirty miles west of Galveston between noon and 8:30 p.m. Winds gusted to 120 miles per hour and the storm tide reached a height of fifty feet between 6-8 A.M. The best estimate is that 6,000 people died and 3,600 homes were destroyed.

Joseph was in Galveston when the storm hit. Sarah was up north visiting Mamie and Short. " During the storm the men of the town, after leaving their wives and children in as much safety as possible, went into the flood areas to assist in rescue work. Harry Hawley left his wife and 5 month old son in their high-raised home on Ave. K and went on such a mission. During his absence the water rose with terrifying rapidity. He was unable to get back to his family. His wife was alone in the house with the prospect of drowning along with her infant son, when she conceived the idea of tying herself and the child to her massive dining room table. It was by this means they were saved from being washed into the swift and deadly flood in the street, and so were rescued. Joseph Henry was able to obtain passage for Harry and family on the S. Savannah, a Lyke's steamer bound for New York. When Mamie greeted her brother in New York the refugees had on the same tattered garments they had worn throughout the flood".

(from notes by Richard 11 and Genevieve)

Joseph checked on the rest of the family: Stella Willis in the P.J. Willis 11 house at the corner of Broadway and Tremont, the house on H Street still owned by Short and Mamie, Narcissa's house on Broadway, damaged, the west side blown out, with many of the beautiful frescoes ruined. Phyllis and Frank Walthew were in that house and made it a place of refuge for all persons during the storm. Josef was able to get off telegrams to Short to keep him informed.

Joseph was appointed Commissioner of The Home Guard, which carried not only the responsibility of safeguarding private property and identifying the dead, but also of disposing of the thousands of corpses. He wrote "I superintended the handling of 500 bodies over the wharves at Galveston on to barges, whence they were taken out to sea with weights attached to them and sunk as only means, at that time, by which they could be disposed of."

    Gary Cartwright in his book <u>Galveston </u>wrote "There were so many bodies that after a while the senses numbed, and the corpses seemed to b e merely some sort of demented design. They were heaped together in the streets, strewn across vacant lots, sticking from mounds of wreckage, floating in shallow pools of the bay. Most were naked, mutilated, and dashed beyond recognition. They hung like macabre ornaments from trees, trestles, and telephone poles."

Joseph wrote "Every man here has nerve and has tried to do his duty – the measure of it was that which he could do. For two days and two nights we stayed up, not knowing even that we were tired, until we could go no further. Instances of courage and heroism are thick, for every man seemed to have the courage necessary to meet such an occasion".

    Josef's letter describing the storm is in The Rosenberg Library in Galveston.

The call for volunteers went out in Montgomery, some 90 miles away, for men to go to the coast with their mules and wagons to help with the gathering up of debris and bodies. The Martin brothers responded, though it is not clear which of the brothers went.

Attending the Republican National Convention as a delegate pledged to Mr. Taft, in Chicago in 1912 was the second big event in his life. His description of the convention and all of the activities is corroborated by Doris Kearns Goodwin in her book <u>The Bully Pulpit.</u> He calls Teddy Roosevelt a socialist, saying "he claims to be a gentleman when his entire bearing and treatment of every subject is that of a thug and bully". Sound familiar? He went to Washington to visit Mamie and family after the convention, and on June 28th had an appointment to meet with President Taft.

Washington Herald, July 27, 1910

    Mrs. Joseph Hawley of Galveston, Texas, who made her home here last winter with Mrs. Short Adam Willis, her daughter, died suddenly yesterday at Spring Lake, N. J., where she had gone to spend the summer with Mrs. Willis. Mrs. Hawley had been in ill health for nearly a year. The internment will be in Luisville, Ky.

Two years later Joseph developed a friendship with a second cousin, Julia Raine, a divorcee from Memphis, Tenn. Marriage was in the wind. On July 15th, 1912 he wrote to Mamie about a meeting between he, Julia and the lawyers in Memphis. "I went to Memphis and stayed two days. During that time the whole matter was worked out by the lawyers and all the property involved scheduled and properly segregated in such form known as Ante - Nuptual Contract so that none of the principal in any form whether stock, bonds or real estate actual money can be exposed to speculation or outside business in any fashion. It formal in every way but all my own rights were fully reserved under the laws of Tenn. and Texas. Julia was there personally and stood the inquiries quite bravely – faced the music finely so it was all sworn to and placed in Escrow with her attys to be filed at the accomplishment of the marriage whereever we may think it best and most convenient to be performed. It was exceedingly gratifying to me to have these instruments drawn up as it renders absolutely all the property from loss by any cause. The lady exhibited a great deal of anticipation over the situation after everything was in order. I left for Texas that same evening."

"I had an interview in the News of today which in every place I go seems to have struck a popular chord. Saw ….at the hotel—they were apparently delighted to hear of you and my sojourn in W. Reflecting thereon, I do think for a man to sit down with a Rear Admiral and a Captain for a luncheon as their guest is a little out of the ordinary. Tell Short that I thank him for his wholesale welcome and his loving treatment."

Washington Herald, September 15th, 1912

A wedding of much interest to Washingtonians, particularly to the Navy set here, is that of Hon. Joseph Hawley of Galveston, Tex., and Mrs. Julia Raine (divorced wife of Gilbert D. Raine of Memphis, Tenn.). Mr. Hawley is the father of Mrs. Short Adam Willis of this city, a charming young matron who has been prominent in Colonial Dames & D.A.R. circles. Mr. Hawley was educated at the Naval Academy at Annapolis. He is well known as one of the leading Taft Republicans in the Lone Star State, and was named a member of the committee appointed to notify Vice President Sherman of his re-nomination at the Chicago convention. Mrs. Raine is a brilliant woman, the author of a number of charming books and plays, and is well known in literary circles. Mr. and Mrs. Hawley will visit Mrs. Willis at her home in Nineteenth Street early in October."

Mamie and Short invited the newlyweds to come to Washington to have Christmas with them. From Galveston Julia wrote "Our seeming neglect has resulted from deep concern coming to both of us, arising from a concatenation of disappointments of various kinds; as well as a no less unexpected series of surprises from different sources. The resulting situations left us with no alternative but to try and work them out, without burdening you with their recitals, until our efforts to overcome them were crowned with success. We are both well, have found very much personal happiness and comfort with each other, and speak of you daily." By 1914 they were divorced.

In 1918 Robert Bradley, Joseph's millionaire brother, gave him a lifetime annuity of $500.00 a month. He retired and until his death lived in Houston in the home of his cousin, Mrs. Pearl Brown Buckingham.

His son wrote of him" At eighty years of age he was as vitally interested in politics and philosophy as he had been in his youth. He was a man of great dignity of bearing, speech and conduct. He was a connoisseur of food, and eating to him was as pleasurable an experience as was the art of conversation."

Joseph Henry Hawley died after suffering a fall and being in a coma for several days. Rosemary, his caretaker, wrote "Harry Hawley was with him constantly from Monday noon until the end. He held his father's hand and knelt by his bed during the last 30 min which brought the end + Peace, Peace. The service was held at home – our friends covered the casket with beautiful flowers—the house was full of our good friends.

There was another brother, Frank Lafayette Hawley, born November 11, 1857, 11 years younger than Joseph Henry. Frank died at age 27 in San Antonio, it is unknown how or why. Josef 's body was cremated. His son Harry, daughter-in-law Susan, and cousin Rosemary took the ashes to San Antonio to be sprinkled in the San Antonio River. We can assume these were his instructions, given to Harry, possibly to fulfill a promise made to Frank.

Joseph Henry Hawley with Olive

JOHN HENRY HAWLEY
SARAH BALL DAVIS

John Henry Hawley, called "Harry", son of Joseph Henry Hawley and Sarah Carter Brown "was a quiet man, a true esthetic by temperament. As a youth he had to work hard to help supplement the family income. His mother was a semi-invalid, his father a radical, his beautiful sister (Mamie) a social pet in a society which the family could ill afford. The boy sold his bicycle to buy the material for the sister's wedding dress. As an adult he was probably best known for his customs brokerage firm, Hawley & Letzerich, which serviced petroleum vessels that came through the Port of Galveston from Mexico" (from notes by Richard 11 and Genevieve)

"His wife, Sarah Ball Davis, was the daughter of the notorious "Carpet Bagger" Governor of Texas. Aunt Sarah was an unusually intelligent woman with high principles and strong determination. Her life was devoted to her home, her children, and the poor and needy of Galveston. She had her own inherited income and owned the property at 2327 Avenue K, which later became "The Virginia Point Inn" Bed and Breakfast. (from notes by Richard 11 and Genevieve).

Their two children were Joseph Henry Hawley, 111 and Sarah Allen Hawley.
    The son, Harry 111, ran away from home in 1913, enlisted in the United States' Cavalry as a private. In 1915, while trying to hitch a ride home from his station in El Paso, he fell between the railroad freight cars and amputated his arm above the elbow. During World War 11, after being rejected by all branches of the service, he volunteered his 200 ft. yacht, his services and financial underwriting for a crew to the United States Coast Guard. His offer was accepted. While on submarine watch in the Gulf off the coast of Mexico he performed heroically and later was awarded a Presidential citation. He married three times, but had no children. When last heard of he was living as a recluse in Brenham with interests in oil painting and travel.

Their daughter, Sarah Allen Hawley "Sally", attended St. Mary's School for Girls in Peekskill, NY and the Scudder School in New York and lived in Ohio after graduation and during her brief marriage to Robert Paul Creson, whom she divorced. They had two children, Paul and Sally, both of whom married and lived in Dallas." (from notes by Richard 11 and Genevieve). Sally was a beautiful, lively, gracious lady, very interested in history and genealogy. I met her when I went to Galveston in 1975. She came and got me off the bus (we were touring), took me to lunch at Gaido's and cried when she spoke of my mother, Olive, her first cousin. She then took me out to her fantastic house to show me a lot of antiques and artifacts related to the family. We kept up correspondence after that. She sent me a copy of the Hawley family history. A couple of years later I contacted her to see if she could help to locate Henry Willis, whose signature was needed on an oil lease. She was no help, as she professed to know nothing. Not two hours after my call her doorbell rang, and there stood Henry Willis, just stopping by to say hello while on a trip to Texas. She directed him to Montgomery and he visited there with several Martin family members. Shortly thereafter Sally fell, broke her hip, and died during surgery. I sincerely regret not having the time to know her better, as she was a most charming, fascinating lady

WILLISTON FARMS

"but the land is always here and the people
who love and understand it are the people who
really own it … for a little while".
　　　　　　　　　　　　　Willa Cather

The land of which we speak is located in Montgomery County, Texas, one mile south of the town of Montgomery, just off FM149. The name Williston Farms came from the Maryland home of Arthur John Willis, uncle of Short Adam.

In early 1914 Short and Mamie made the decision to leave Washington. D.C. and settle in Montgomery on land that Short had inherited. The property was put in Mamie's name and she carefully sought quitclaim deeds from all family members. In January land for a right-of-way from the property to the public road (FM 149) was purchased. Mamie hired the services of a Washington, D.C. architectural firm to draw up plans for the home to be built on this land. By March those plans were ready. Written on the front of the plans is " to be located near Galveston, Texas. " In reality, it was 90 miles from Galveston, over very poor roads— a challenging journey. That same month (March)a six-month's lease was signed on a house in Galveston at the corner of Broadway and 27th Street owned by Short's niece Laura Jackson. Short Adam remained in Washington – Mamie was in charge of the family and the construction project. Richard Short 11 and Henry Hawley were placed in school in Galveston. Their governess, Miss Nash, who came from Washington with the family, assumed charge of the Galveston home. Olive Elizabeth was kept under her mother's surveillance." (from notes by Richard 11 and Genevieve)

In order to supervise the construction, Mamie and Olive rented a room in the home of the local doctor in Montgomery. Since Olive was on the market, it is assumed that there were frequent trips to Galveston to attend social events - how else could she meet a prospect?

On a trip to Sea Island, Georgia I spent a day on Jekyll Island touring restored homes. I was immediately struck by the resemblance of those houses to "the big house" in Montgomery, down to the detail of the tiles and fixtures in the bathrooms. Doing some research I found that the floor plan of "the big house" is that of the "single house", the prevailing floor plan for the historic houses of Charleston, virtually unheard of in any other city. "With gable end to the street, one room in width and two rooms in depth, divided by a central stair hall, the single house was recorded in its earliest form around 1700.

Born in "the big house", and living there the first six years of my life, this is how I remember it. It was big—two huge rooms, enormous in scale – (the best estimate is 40 to 50 ft.), with high ceilings, separated by a wide hall and reception area that accommodated the front entrance that faced north. Three small windows were placed vertically on either side of the front door. On the outside there was a pediment over the front door with a porte-cochere and a circular driveway approaching it. The gable end of the house faced east and the street, which was FM 149, a good ½ mile away. The exterior walls were painted white, with the exception of the front east wall, which was pink brick. Upon entering the front door you immediately are confronted by a door to the right, opening to a flight of stairs leading down to underground storage. Just outside, to the right of the front door, was a large metal trap-door where supplies could be lowered for storage. This was the idea of architects who lived in the northern, drier climate. In east Texas, with its heavy rainfall, the storage area stayed full of water, thus rendered unusable. It not only was a breeding place for mosquitos, if you opened the door you looked down to see snakes swimming in the water.

Turn right at the front door, go down a short hall and you find a small room that served as an office, with windows facing north and a powder room (sink and toilet).

Looking straight ahead from the front door you are surrounded by beautiful wood paneling. When the house was demolished in 1955 a bill of lading was found indicating that this paneling was virgin pine from North Carolina, which cost $600 per carload. Both the house and the barn were built of this pine, so it must have taken many carloads. (In 1914 $600 had the purchasing power of $10,590.58 in 2001). Floors were also tongue-in-groove pine. Ceilings were tall – 12 – 14 ft. Continuing down the hall you came upon a stairway that went up – headed north, then a small landing with a double window facing over the porte-cachere, than another section of stairway doubling back to lead to the upstairs hall.
    To the east were French doors leading to the drawing room, to the right French doors leading to the living room. And straight ahead double French doors leading outside.

Turning left you entered the drawing room --a room of enormous proportions (I remember roller-skating in this room). All the walls were wood paneling, with a line of French doors on the south leading outside, a plain wall on the west side, a north wall with bookshelves, centered with four windows and a window seat, and an east wall centered with a huge fireplace flanked by French doors on either side leading to the front porch.

The porch had white columns (which eventually rotted out from the moisture and humidity and were replaced with brick columns), a brick wall and floor, serving as a carport. The brick walkway began at this porch and ran all along the south side of the house, about 3 ft. wide, topped with a pergola covered with bougainvillea.

Turning right (or west) from the entrance hall you entered another enormous room, a duplicate of the other in size -south wall French doors leading out to the walkway, west wall a fireplace flanked by French doors Leading to a glassed in porch. It had a smaller back-to-back fireplace, a back door to outside, and a swinging door on the north wall that led to the dining room.

The dining room was a normal size. On the south was a row of built-in cabinets with glass fronts – windows on the west wall – a swinging door on the north wall led to the kitchen.. On the east wall a staircase that went up a short way, a landing with a north window, then doubling back to go up to the second floor, another landing on the second floor, a short passageway to the right, then straight up to the attic. Underneath that staircase in the dining room was a closet for coats and shoes.

The kitchen was small with the sink along the east wall with windows above it, the stove on the north wall. The west wall had two windows and a door that led outside.

The second floor was laid out along a hall that ran the length of the house, east to west. On the East end was the upstairs porch, the master bedroom which included a fireplace flanked by French doors, windows to the south and north, a small dressing room, closet and bathroom. The hall then went past the staircase landing, three bedrooms in a row, and at the west end another suite of bedroom with fireplace flanked by French doors leading to a small porch. On the north side of that hall were two bathrooms and closets. At the west end of that hall was the staircase that led up to the attic or down to the dining room.

The attic was huge, running the full length of the house, open with the fireplace chimneys that stood like soldiers and went straight up through the roof. It was not dark—there were vents and little dormer windows on the north and south sides – but it was scary because there was a huge chicken snake that hung out up there – you would catch glimpses of him slithering along the rafters - supposedly he was a good guy because he ate all the rats.

The fireplaces were all the same pink brick, Ferris, made in Texas, and used for the chimneys and the walkways that ran along the south side of the house. The fireplaces were massive, of simple design, with a ledge mantel.

When the house was built there was a battery shed just outside the kitchen, filled with Delco etc. Those were no longer in use when Stump and Olive moved in.

The huge barn sat some distance from the house. It was built of the same virgin pine as the house with a tin roof. On the west end there were stables below for the horses, with pens and a dipping vat adjoining. The upstairs was for storage of hay, etc. Next to the barn there was a windmill and a large cistern, a well house, and a smokehouse. There were seven tenant houses, two within sight of "the big house."

By early 1915 the house and farm were completed. Short Adam arrived from Washington with his nurse and four boxcars of belongings. Williston Farms became their official residence.

Montgomery was a very small community of mostly farmers, isolated, outnumbered by the black population and very provincial in their attitude. They were amazed and amused at this woman who arrived to build this huge house, throw money around and proceed to set up a farming operation when it was obvious she knew nothing about farming, only what she could glean from bulletins she ordered from Texas A & M. The barn she built was bigger and more elaborate than most of the local homes. Using a bank of Delco Batteries she had electricity and running water, with indoor toilets that worked – another luxury enjoyed by few if any of the locals. She acquired a herd of Jersey cows with the intention of establishing a dairy, hoping to produce butter she could sell to the hotels in Houston. Reading that cows produced more butter if their drinking water was cool, to the astonishment of the locals she ordered the help to dump ice into the water troughs. She planted and grew asparagus, which the locals had never heard of, much less eaten or grown. She ran an ad in the local paper to hire someone to manage the place, hiring the husband of one of the local teachers, thus establishing a direct line for the spread of gossip about her through the community. Her husband was sick and disabled--she was a woman operating in a man's world ---and her haughty, autocratic attitude did not endear her to those who dealt with her. In her contact with local trades people it is thought she probably did some business with Stump Martin a local trader in horses and mules, who was to play an important role in her life as a fierce adversary.

Short, Mamie's husband, died in November 1917. In March of 1918 she was considering putting the place on the market. She asked for an appraisal from the architect, receiving a telegram saying it should bring at least $175,000.00. batteries used to provide electricity, lighting,

In November of 1918 she turned over 507 acres of Williston Farms to Stump, retaining for herself the house, outbuilding and 20 acres of land. Her career as a farmer was over.

Hanging over her head was a loan she had taken out with the Federal Land Bank program. By 1925 she had missed several payments on that loan and was facing bankruptcy. To their credit those in charge of the loan were reluctant to see this property lost to the family, but were realistic enough to face the facts. One official writes "It would be a great pity to see this farm, with its splendid improvements, pass out of the family, though I recognize the fact that unless occupied by an owner and used and developed along business lines, the revenues from it will continue to be disappointing." Getting nowhere with Mamie, they appealed to Stump." I understand that you are a man of sound business judgment, and that your wife is a daughter of Mrs. Willis. I would regret to see this farm foreclosed and the property lost to the family, I understand that the land is of fair quality, some of it running from grey to black, and have seen the improvements on the place. While they are more expensive than good judgment would require, from the standpoint of the needs of the farm and probably represent a cost equal to, or greater than, the value of the land. Yet such improvements increase greatly the market value of the farm."

Stump and Olive bailed her out, paying off the loan. They agreed to give her 5 years to try to sell the place and possibly salvage some of her money.

One official of the Land Bank program wrote "She naturally feels and believes that the farm should have a value equal to the value of the land and cost of the improvements, On the other hand, there are comparatively few people able to buy who would be interested in so well improved a farm as this, therefore the difficulty of making a sale at a fair price". (i.e. she spent too much money on the place)

She ran an ad in <u>The New York Times</u>:

"TEXAS 528 acre farm, best land, shareholding crops, no overflow, splendid climate, abundant woods, artesian well 50,000 gallons, good roads, 2 miles from town and station. Every convenience. 16 buildings, new, beautiful 17 room residence, 4 baths, 60 Delco batteries, silo, engines, machinery, tools. Price $????. No trades. Easy terms, Mrs. Short Willis Montgomery, Texas."

Mamie left Montgomery in early 1927.

September 1, 1930 was the date on which the contract would end and Mamie would lose the property. In June of that year Mamie, living in New Jersey, began correspondence with lawyers about the contract. She suspicioned that Stump had signed an oil lease, concealed it from her, and not paid her fair share. Although several tried to reason with her, she would listen to no one.

An attorney from a law firm in Houston wrote Mamie in 1930, pointing out that had not Stump come up with the $7,500 five years earlier the property would have been lost then. "You say that you do not wish to sue him over any oil rental money which may have been received…neither do you wish to offend them. Under the circumstances, I know of no surer way to offend both your daughter and her husband than to have some lawyer whom they do not know write, making a demand in behalf of the mother and mother-in-law."

In 1930 there was an exchange of letters between Mamie, Olive and Stump. Mamie wrote saying she could not get a bidder on the property unless she advertised, and that would necessitate the publication of Stump's supposed agreement with an oil company, which, she says, has never been recorded since obviously the Company would have required her signature and would have paid her half of the rentals." Would they like her to turn the matter over to a lawyer?"

Olive wrote her Mother saying Stump has no objection to her advertising, or to turning it over to a lawyer. The lawyer intervened, and Stump's reply, written by Olive but signed by him, was "If I am not mistaken you want to make this settlement on Mrs. Willis' contention and statements, ignoring the contract entirely. I could have bought this place for less money and without any tail tied to it, but I did not consider it worth the money. But I was persuaded by Mrs. Willis and her friends that it was my duty to make the trade we made. I was led to believe that, situated as she was, she could make a sale before the contract expired, that would save her considerable loss and also make me some money.

When the place was turned over to me it was badly run down and I have spent considerable money in clearing the land, building fences and putting the land in a general state of cultivation in order to make it attractive to any buyer she secured. I have also made every reasonable effort to make a sale myself. She still has six months on the life of this contract and I am willing to assist you or anyone else she thinks would be a help in making a sale.

In other words, I want to live up to the contract from A to Z.

The only effort she has made, as far as I (can see) know to save herself any loss is an offer thro you that I consider so unjust and unfair and so far out of line with the contract that it does not deserve any consideration whatever.

Yours truly, I.L. Martin per O.W.M."

The lawyer followed up with a new contract, which was promptly returned with a note: "Enclosed find contract. I cannot afford to sign an extension of the contract after the unreasonable demands you have made on the old one. Yours truly," signed Stump Martin per O.W.M.

Not to be deterred, Mamie proceeded to have the lawyer make demands on Stump by registered letter and file a lawsuit in Federal Court "to have the deed reformed and contract entered into between you and her." The court ruled in favor of Stump. On September 1, 1930, with negotiations over, Stump and Olive officially owned the property, thus marking the end of Williston Farms.

Stump and Olive had moved into "the big house" in 1927 with their four children. Two more children would be born to them there—a girl, Rose Marie, in July 1927 and another girl, Olive Elizabeth, in April, 1930.

With the death of Olive and Stump, the three older siblings had Stump's Will set aside and bought out the interest of the three younger heirs. In 1955 "the big house" and barn were torn down, the materials salvaged and used to construct homes for the two brothers.

In the years since, with the expansion of Houston to the north and the development of Lake Conroe as a recreational area, the Montgomery of Mamie, Olive, and Stump's time (and my memory) has disappeared. Small portions of the original acreage are still owned by next generations of the family, including 217 acres established as a nature preserve. The site of "the Big House" is now a horse farm owned by someone out of Houston.

Our family owned it ....
"for a little while".

CHAPTER 6

6th *Generation*

OLIVE ELIZABETH WILLIS

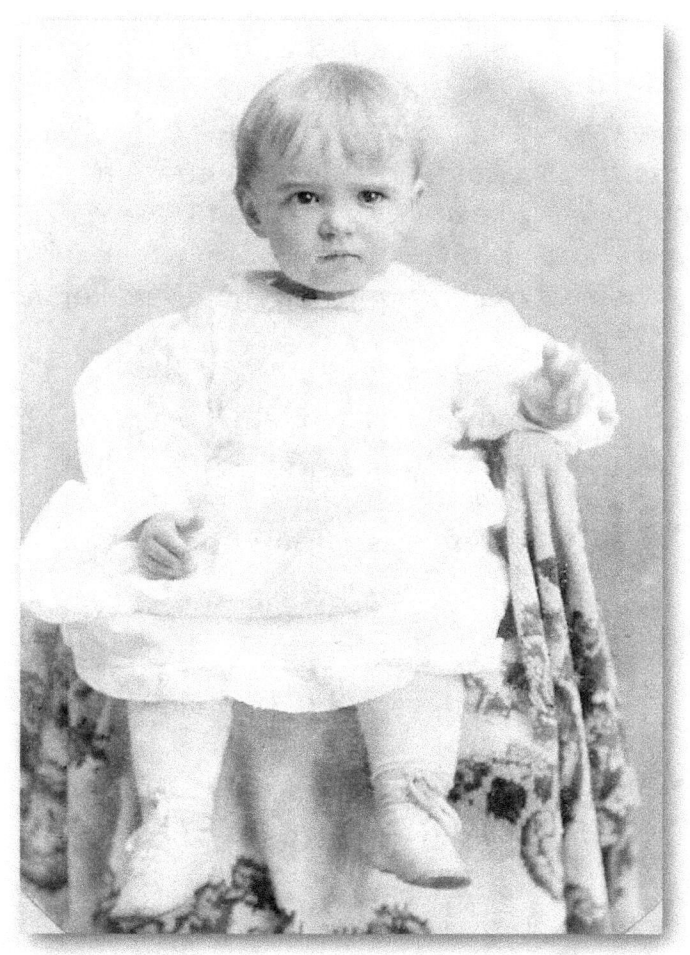

"I REMEMBER EVERYTHING THAT HAPPENED in far away Galveston - - so long ago. The sun shown warm and bright, the garden was full of flowers, there were over a hundred roses in the house because I cut all of our own and filled every bowl and vase and the gardener brought a hamper full at two o'clock, he was a German and very superstitious & presented them to "My Lady for good luck and a happy baby" and you came late in the afternoon, so pretty & fat and sweet with your tiny hands wide open. Reba said that showed you were born generous and candid. We were so glad to have you, darling. No little one was ever more welcome or more heartily loved, and your dear place in our hearts and lives can never be less. (Olive, away at boarding school, received this letter describing her birth on her 15th birthday, May 3rd, 2010. It was signed "Ever the same loving Mother, Mary H. Willis")

Olive Elizabeth Willis was born May 3rd, 1895 to Mary Carter Hawley Willis, age 24, and Short Adam Willis, age 47. They had been married 14 months. She was born in the upstairs bedroom on the right at 1416 H. Street in Galveston, Texas and baptized at Trinity Church. By November of that year, when Olive was six months old, the family was living in New York City. Mamie turned the care of her child over to a series of nurses while she engaged in social activities and traveling. Delia, pictured with Olive at age one, was only the first of a succession of caretakers. In a letter dated December, 1896, when Olive was 19 months old, Short wrote to Mamie who was off on a trip "The kid is jolly as a Sand Piper and has all the amusement she wants. The weather continues to freeze and it makes the kid look like a rosey moon faced Dutch Baby – all except the China blue eyes".

In March of 1904 Mamie was off on a shopping trip when Olive wrote her a note telling of her good marks and one bad mark from Rose, the caretaker, and wishing mother good weather for shopping.

By the time she was five they had moved to Litchfield, Conn. They lived first on South Street, but when Olive was seven her brother Richard was born, followed by Henry when she was eight. That necessitated a move to a larger house, and this time they had acreage, with a barn, a pony, chickens, etc. There were lots of pets –a little dog, a striped cat and a horse named Texas.

In 1907 Mamie took all three children to Asbury Park, New Jersey to recover from the whooping cough. Short wrote "I am so glad Olive had "such a time". You (Mamie) are so busy telling about her that you entirely neglected to mention the boys. I suppose it is natural for a mother to renew her youth in admiration for her first young lady. Perhaps in time Olive will learn to be more of a girl and less of a cowboy. It will come out all right in time". Olive was 12 at this time—this is the first criticism of her – a hint that she was not the perfect daughter – and a suggestion that her mother was doting on her to the detriment of the two boys).)

At thirteen Olive was allowed to go by steamer from New York to Galveston for a visit with her Grandfather and Grandmother Hawley. Grandfather wrote to Mamie "Olive arrived at 7 a.m. Her manner is almost totally yours. She is grown indeed for one so young. You know, of course, she is intensely like you in face. Her hair is simply lovely – it is not so long as was yours, but it seems intensely like you in every other aspect. I know we are going to be the dearest friends."

"We can get very good horses here and, as Olive has her riding habit, she can see something of the country with me. She told me this morning that an ordinary Mexican saddle would do. We are going to get along famously".

"Assure Short that his daughter is altogether lovely and will, in due time, will come back to him greatly improved physically and I hope mentally. She said this morning, in a very firm manner, her intention to return to New York on the same steamer Nueces on some future voyage, saying " You see Grandfather it takes three days at least to know the proper officers, and if I go back by the Nueces I now know them and that will be all done away with and I can get right down to enjoying the trip". This shows observation and management."(Again a hint of a problem when he says she will return greatly improved physically and hopefully mentally).

Henry, Olive's younger brother, says in one of his letter that he remembers when they sent Olive off to a convent in Baltimore. The letter written to her on her fifteenth birthday is sent to Mount de Sales –The school is a Catholic girl's boarding school, run by The Sisters of Visitation with the goal of helping and educating young women and turning girls into leaders—as they phrased it – -" the education of the heart". Located just outside Baltimore, it was a Greek Revival structure with many, many stairs and a cupola on top from which you could see Baltimore Harbor. Olive was not doing well—her Mother writes "Speaking of success, don't worry one bit over the marks. Mother wants them to be good only as an indication that you are honestly trying to lead your life rightly. If a question is asked which you do not know, just make a mental note "This is something to be learned". And remember, I sent you to Mount de Sales to acquire something much more important than any facts. I fancy you know what I mean, but will put it into words. " to be <u>sweet</u> and <u>obedient</u>". I feel sure you understand Mother's anxiety for your development and realize my great love for my darling"."". She goes on to promise her a pony—"a direct reward for the beautiful spirit of effort to meet the requirements and prove yourself worthy of our pride in your character". She then says "God will bless us all, dear, if we keep on trying to do His will and make one another good and happy". (The year at boarding school was obviously a move meant to punish and reform a rebellious teenager.)

It seems Olive was only at Mount de Sales for a year. She is pictured on her horse (maybe the pony she was promised as a reward) in Washington, D.C. on September20, 2011, by which date the school term would be underway.

Probably she was enrolled at Gunston Hall in 1911 as a Freshman - we know she was there in 1912 as a Sophomore, scheduled to graduate in 1914. Gunston Hall was located in Washington, D.C and was "foremost among Washington's institutions for higher education of girls and young ladies, a school planned for those who desire the best advantages and wish a beautiful and cultured home, refined associations, and able instruction "– These were exactly Mamie's goals for her daughter.

Mamie wrote of her "Olive is the prettiest 16 year old in Washington". Meantime, there is a hint of a flirtation between Olive and a chauffeur, which set off alarm bells for Mamie— it was time to get her married off to a "suitable" prospect. The Willis family had only been living in Washington, D.C. for some five years. Although Mamie had connections through the D.A.R., and Short had friends in government and political circles, they turned to family connections in Galveston, through the Willis and Hawley relatives. Mamie and Olive went to Galveston for two months. It is difficult to tell just who was making the debut---Olive or Mamie –as Mamie demanded her share of the spotlight - and you can well imagine how difficult it must have been for Olive to be put "on parade" among people she barely knew. For the next two years after her debut, when the social season began, Mamie would take Olive to Galveston to pursue the hunt. Olive told her son John there were two serious candidates – a doctor from Galveston and an older Senator from Kentucky, widowed with three children. She was not interested in either of them.

When they returned to Washington, it was announced they would be moving to Texas. Olive's life was to be uprooted—she had lived in Connecticut and Washington since she was a baby, and now they were moving not only to far-away Texas, but to an isolated spot in the middle of nowhere. Furthermore, Mamie insisted that Olive stay with her --- under her surveillance - -- living in Montgomery for the months it took to construct the house and farm. When you look at the picture of Olive, , you can see a look of rebellion and defiance on her face, made more obvious by her body language.

In early 1915, construction was completed. Short arrived from Washington, D.C. with four carloads of household goods and his nurse. Williston Farms was now their home.

A reluctant Olive arrives.

This was a storm brewing that Mamie, in her focus on her own goals, did not sense. It was only natural that Olive would pass the time in the activity she loved the most---riding -- with the animals who had been her closest friends since childhood -- –horses - on the vast acreage and out of sight. Her brother Richard 11wrote "Olive – in her new found freedom – was completely happy and indifferent to her mother's problems. She loved to wander alone on horseback over the beautiful countryside, to fish in the streams, to hunt, to pursue her deep love – drawing – she was an exceptional natural artist with an artist's deep under- standing of nature." It is surely in this way that she met, became friends with, and eventually fell in love with Stump Martin. In spite of the difference in their backgrounds and ages, he offered her an escape from an overpowering, domineering Mother, and the plans her mother had mapped out for her life.. The fact that she inherited a small fortune from her grandmother, Narcissa, empowered her—it was her key to freedom.

On August 14th, 1915 Stump and Olive rode over to the town of Anderson in neighboring Grimes County and were married by the Justice of the Peace. It is not known how long they kept the marriage secret, but evidently a pregnancy made it necessary to face her mother and father. The scene that followed was an ugly one, indeed. Olive lost the baby from that pregnancy - (stress?) – but in May, 1917 she delivered her first child, naming the girl Narcissa Willis, for the grandmother who left her a legacy and thus bought her freedom. Her father, Short, died in September of that year. His prediction, made when Olive was twelve, "perhaps in time Olive will learn to be more of a girl and less of a cowboy. It will work out all right in time" did not come true. The breach between Olive and her mother never healed. Henry Willis, who was very fond of his big sister, said he had to sneak off to see her because their mother was so vehement in her bitterness.

The couple lived in a house located some miles further out from the town - further back up in the woods. You can just imagine the adjustments they had to make – to each other, to their new circumstances. It had to be difficult for each of them—Olive because she was living in a very different world, totally isolated from everything she had known.

The "Dick Womack" house, home of Olive and "Stump" until they moved to "the big house" at Williston Farms in 1926-27. Their first four children wer born in this house. Pictured are John and Pete on the bigger horse, Mary Jo and Narcissa on the smaller horse.

Stump because he was no longer a bachelor and had to accept new responsibilities and learn to understand this beautiful, spoiled, childlike young woman who had come into his life. She knew nothing (and did not want to know anything) about housekeeping, cooking, any of the practical skills that are involved in daily living., so the responsibility fell back on him. Added to that were the pregnancies—they had four children in seven years – Narcissa Willis – 1917, John Willis – 1919, Isaac Lafayette, Jr. – 1922, Mary Josephine – 1924. These were the years that formed their relationship with each other and with their children.

Their lives changed dramatically in 1927. Mamie left Montgomery and Olive and Stump moved into "the big house". Shortly thereafter their fifth child, Rose Marie, was born, to be followed three years later in 1930, by their sixth, Olive Elizabeth.

Olive was not a homemaker and was an indifferent mother (patterned after Mamie) – she left the care and nurturing of the children to the black help or their father, just as her mother had done. Rose Marie tells of trying to get ready for school one morning. It had been raining, and since the children had to walk out to the main road to catch the bus she was trying to find her rain boots, which were kept in the closet under the stairs in the dining room. She could only find one boot and, in desperation, she went to her mother, who was sitting at the table reading something, and appealed to her for help. Her mother turned to her and said

"Why child, I have no idea where it is" and went back to her reading. That was her attitude toward the children and their care. She would read to them, she would play games with them, she would sit and let them brush her hair, but only at her pleasure. They could not turn to her in need. They quickly learned to go instead to the help or to their father, who, if he was around, was most concerned and caring. Her oldest daughter, Narcissa, who was 16 when her mother died, and thus had the longest relationship with her mother, spoke of her only with scorn.

Olive's soul mate was her oldest son, John—he was the most like the Willis side of the family, they shared many interests, and enjoyed each other's company. The second son and the second and fourth girls resembled the Martins in build, in appearance, and certainly in stubbornness. The third girl was unique : quite small when born and somewhat fragile. Mamie, in a letter to her father, written July 29, 1927, says "A letter from Olive – full of such wonderful news. Harry (Olive's uncle) had been up there and the baby was born an hour after he left & she is lovely and quite well and Olive had ice cream for supper & says having babies is no trouble at all. So she is like me in body anyway." Olive named the baby Rose Marie, after her favorite doll from her childhood.

Olive was petite with luxurious black hair, an olive complexion and green eyes. Everyone said she was a very beautiful woman. Her brother and his wife, who knew her well, wrote this appraisal of her: "Olive Willis Martin was a woman of great personal charm and beauty who spent her entire life defying convention. She had no patience with snobbery, hypocrisy, or lies. She was truthful to the point of bluntness. She sincerely respected the individuality of everyone, regardless of creed or color, and demanded the same for herself. Her loyalty to her husband and children never waivered, but she refused to smother them with love or rob them of self-reliance. To amuse her children she drew boats, battleships under full rigging, horses, animals of all kinds and the landscapes familiar to them. For her own amusement she would read, spend hours in target knife throwing, shooting or, perhaps camp in the woods by herself overnight. Housework, cooking, or sewing bored her. Though she would work cattle at the side of her husband, she built her own world around her family and her own dreams. She asked nothing of the world beyond."(as written by Richard 11 and Genevieve – her brother and sister-in-law).

She did not mix or mingle with the local ladies. It is said she considered their gossip silly, preferring to read or follow her own pursuits. She indulged herself. She always had a car of some sort, usually a truck, though Stump never learned to drive. She would go to town and buy what the locals, who could only afford the bare necessities in those hard times of the thirties, considered very indulgent foods (stuffed olives, mushrooms, maraschino cherries, sardines, chocolate candy). Both Olive and Stump smoked –she smoked "store bought Lucky Strike", he rolled his own with "Prince Albert" tobacco in a can. The one constant element in her life was a horse - Olive always had a horse from childhood (Texas) to the day of her death(Choctaw).. I was told that one of the black help asked her one day "Miss Olive, why did you marry Mr. Stump?" "Because I liked the lifestyle" was her answer.

Olive had a very volatile temper. The children witnessed her in the dining room eating sardines from a can. Stump came in and made a teasing comment that offended her. She picked up a pitcher of milk and poured it over his head. John, her oldest son, who seemed to be her favorite, was sitting at the end of the table and said something she did not like. She picked up a knife and threw it at him. Luckily, he ducked. The knife went through the back of the chair. Knife throwing was one of her hobbies—she practiced it regularly. One of the younger girls was sitting in the car with her mother in town one day. A local teenager walked up to the car and said something to Olive, who, without hesitation, slapped her!

She was friends with her brother Richard and his wife Genevieve. Gen tells the story of a day in 1930 when Olive arrived at their home in Houston to visit: "She was dressed in a torn and outdated housedress, topped by a large garden-party hat and wearing canvas shoes. John was with her, wearing soiled jeans and shirt, cowboy boots and hat, both of which were two sizes too large. They arrived in a truck in which they had been hauling calves. Olive was radiantly happy to have this day in the city and unconcerned about her appearance. She announced that she was taking Genevieve to lunch at the Terrace Room of the Ritz Hotel, at that time the smartest dining spot in Houston. She was so happy and so confidant, it was impossible to refuse. So Genevieve, John, and Olive piled into the filthy truck, parked in the hotel garage, and had a most delightful and happy luncheon with Houston's elite staring in wonder. This sort of thing amused Olive --"the sham of so-called society".

The children relate that Olive and Stump truly loved each other. They had long and loud arguments, they kidded and joked a lot, but they were demonstrably affectionate toward each other. They spent hours together on horseback – Rose Marie remembers the two of them riding up one evening from somewhere, each of them holding baby lambs who had been orphaned and rescued, brought home to be bottle-fed and raised as pets for the children. For the children Olive recited poetry, drew pictures, and read stories aloud. Stump would often in the evening sing gospel and folksongs. With six children the house, big as it was, sheltered the lives and love of a family On June 17th, 1934, Olive was pregnant with her seventh child. Stump and most of the workers were on the far side of the property, working cattle. She decided to go for a ride on her favorite horse, Choctaw. One of the tenants said "Miss Olive rode up to her house very upset and crying. She asked to be helped down off the horse and told the woman to send someone up to "the big house" and tell them to bring a wagon to get her". They came for her and sent someone into town for the doctor and to fetch Stump. Dr. Young had delivered all of her babies, but after examining her he said they had to get her to the hospital in Houston. While waiting for the ambulance to come, they put her on a cot and carried her down to the entrance hall. She was bleeding profusely. The children were brought in to say goodbye. She bled to death before the ambulance could come, the little girl baby dying in her womb. Stump grabbed his shotgun and started out to shoot Choctaw, but the men restrained him until Dr. Young could make him understand that her death was not caused by the horse, but was a result of the pregnancy.

Stump said to his children "You've lost the best friend you'll ever have. When we lost her we lost the whole world."

Olive was 39 years old when she died. She and Stump were married for 19 years.

ISAAC LAFAYETTE "STUMP" MARTIN

"Stump" Martin was born in Montgomery, Texas on May 14th, 1881, the son of John Martin and Josephine Gaines Moore. His grandfather, Anthony Martin, born in Baden, Germany in 1799, started his journey to America, only to be shipwrecked, surviving in a lifeboat that landed in Nova Scotia. He eventually worked his way to Pennsylvania. At age 32 he married Mary Habermaker, a native of Comstock, France who had come to America with her Catholic parents. Mary had received her diploma as a medical nurse in Colfax, France.

Anthony and Mary with their three children started their journey to Texas in 1839. Stopping in Montgomery to visit friends from Pennsylvania, Anthony purchased 30 acres of land four miles east of Montgomery and established a tannery, which they operated until the 1860's. Anthony died in 1894, Mary in 1897. They and 10 of the eleven children are buried at the home place on the side of Hwy. 105.

Two sons, John and Claiborne, fought in the Civil War. Upon returning from the war they found that the tannery had been forced out of business for lack of materials. They went into partnership farming and raising cattle and began acquiring acreage south of Montgomery at Spring Branch. Claiborne died in 1891, having never married. John married Josephine Gaines Moore in 1876 and produced six sons:: John William (Will), Joseph Benson (Buck), Isaac Lafayette (Stump), Anthony Henry, George Lewis, and Andrew John (Dock). The graves of all six are in "Martin Hill" the family cemetery on F 149.

The Anthony Martin Cemetery

Located just off 105 between Montgomery and Conroe, this is a dedicated cemetery. The family has cleared and fenced the area and restored and replaced the markers. Buried here are our first Martin ancestors in Texas.

Mary Ann Martin
Born in Crepstahl, France
On March 6, 1811
Died Dec 6, 1847
"Dear Mother, we love
Thee in the funeral grave made over
that thy memory will be cherished
until we see this heavenly love"

Anthony Martin
Born in Baden, Germany
On June 13, 1779
Died Oct 26, 1848

Stump's father died when he was 23, leaving the mother widowed with a two year old child. It is thought this is why none of the boys married until late – they had to help support the family. Stump only went to the third grade, and his school year ran from October through February because in the other months he had to work in the fields. He could read and sign his name, but did not write or do math. In all of his negotiations with Mamie and/or lawyers, Olive wrote the letters and he signed them. (He made up for this with his craftiness—when his two older children learned math in school he would have them do the figuring when they were having a livestock sale – how many cows - how much they weighed - how much they would bring at so much per lb. When they had done the multiplying and dividing and came up with a final estimate, they would take it to him only to find that he already had that number, or very close to it, written on a piece of paper – he had done all the figuring in his head). He became involved in the buying and selling of horses and mules, and was very successful because of his shrewdness. He had a very strong work ethic, demanding much of his older children and workers, but always working along side them. He did not go to church, but lived by rigid moral standards and ethics (never worked on Sundays and was a teetotaler). He was very firm in his convictions, could not be swayed (the stubborn factor) but was always fair. All these characteristics made him a worthy opponent to Mamie.

Stump was a big man – over six feet tall. At the time of his marriage to Olive he was quite handsome – tall – well built, with unusually beautiful deep blue eyes which gave one the feeling of ease. Richard 11, his future brother-in-law wrote of him "he was a born opportunist and a crafty trader."

When they first married he was earning his living by buying and selling large quantities of horses and mules for work stock. After gaining possession of Williston he ran a herd of cattle, offered butchering services to local markets and railroad crews, shipped flowers (bluebells) to nurseries in Houston, and had a farming operation that raised cotton, corn and feed grains. He furnished land, food, and housing for black tenant families (sharecroppers) who worked "thirds", fourths", and "halves" on his land. He thus was able to provide for his family (and for those tenant families who were dependent on him) through those tough depression years. Over the years he gradually increased the number of acres he owned. All this on a third grade education!

The name Stump doesn't seem to fit this very macho description, however, there is a story. First of all you have to realize how strong the tradition of "nicknames" was in the local culture. It went back to slavery times, when nicknames were often used by slaves to fool the master. In Montgomery, almost everyone had a nickname—we three little girls were "Flapper" for Mary Jo because she liked to play dress up, "Hoopie" for Rose Marie because she loved the sound of a distant train, and "Tucker" for Olive Elizabeth because of her favorite song – "Old Dan Tucker". These names were given them by the help.

When Isaac Lafayette Martin was about 12 years old he attended a week - long church revival (a tradition harking back to the camp meetings that were popular back in the early 1800's). After a week of preaching and working the crowd into a frenzie, the preacher would march everyone down to the river and baptize them by dunking them. Everyone would be singing, praying, and lining up to be dunked. Isaac sat on a stump on the other side of the creek to watch the goings on. When everyone had been baptized, the preacher turned and called Isaac to come forward. He shook his head and refused to budge, even though others in the congregation pleaded for him to do so. He sat on that stump until everyone went away, and from that day forward he was known to one and all as Stump Martin. It also gave him a life-long reputation for stubbornness.

In December 1934 Stump signed his Will. His brother, J.B. Martin, and oldest daughter, Narcissa, were appointed co-executors of his estate. In return for relinquishing to Buck any claim he mighty have on land owned by his mother and father, he established a Trust, with Buck as trustee, to support and maintain the children. Buck was named as guardian of the three minor children.

It is interesting that he also provided that "should my deceased wife's mother, Mrs. Mary H. Willis, desire to make her home with any of my children upon the lands hereinabove mentioned, it is my will, and I hereby direct said trustee to permit her to do so, and, in such event, to provide for her support and maintenance to the same extent and in the same manner that he has been directed herein to provide for the support of my said children."

Despite the bitterness of their relationship, he felt an obligation to offer to care for her in her old age – just as he had cared for his widowed mother and family throughout his life – he was a man of character.

Three years later, on March 11, 1937 Stump died in the hospital with pneumonia. He would have been 56 that May.

L-R: Huck Hosford of Tillis Prarie, I.L. "Stump" Martin with his trading stock horses and sitting Dave Bishop of Spring Branch. Circa 1900's

Stump and Olive are buried side-by-side in the Martin family cemetery. The tombstone over their grave has the image of a cow, a horse, and their brand---even in her grave Olive has a horse nearby.

RICHARD SHORT WILLIS II
GENEVIEVE MURPHY

When Richard was born a friend wrote Mamie "so few have just what they want, and you have just done it all around". Mamie was 30 years old, Short was 53 and with Olive, their daughter, seven years old they surely were hoping to get a boy. Richard's grandfather Hawley visited when he was six months old and wrote in his usual effusive way "That boy is something wonderful. I truly believe he is the most beautiful boy I ever saw. I believe he will grow up strong – an athlete in physique and a brainy chap who with a University Education and good luck will make a great place for himself in the world …I'm telling all about cousin Richard with his big black eyes".

Richard S. Willis was born April 20, 1902 in Litchfield, Connecticut. Seventeen months later his little brother, Henry Hawley Willis was born, August 10th, 1903. Being so close together the two boys were lumped together in all things, though they could not have been more different in appearance and personality.

Richard inherited the Hawley genes. He was a very handsome man, a very large man, outgoing, gregarious, quite verbal, given to sarcasm, with an infectious laugh. Like his grandfather, he was plagued throughout his life by financial insecurity.

Both boys had the handicap of being raised as "crown princes" in a life of luxury, then abruptly left with no father (Richard was 15, Henry 13 when Short died), no financial security (about this time the money ran out) and a Mother who was on an emotional roller coaster, generously handing out guilt trips at every turn. No surprise that the relationship between the two boys was not good. After graduating from Stanton Military Academy in Virginia, they went their separate ways.

Richard tried a couple of jobs after Stanton, joining the Air Corps Training Program at Kelly Field in San Antonio in 1925. Later that same year he eloped with Genevieve Murphy from El Paso, which meant he was kicked out of the program and disqualified for Wings or Commission. He ultimately joined The Reserve Officers Corps and was given the Commission of Second Lieutenant on Flying Status. There followed a series of moves and jobs: Their first child, Jane, was born in El Paso in 1927, the second, Richard 111, in San Antonio in 1929, and the third, William Edward, in El Paso in 1933. Genevieve had persistent medical problems throughout her life and, possibly due to her Irish heritage, fought an ongoing battle with her private demons. She was a loyal wife, a devoted mother, and a caring friend.

In 1936, in the heart of the depression, they left the children with Mamie in El Paso and went to Houston and Galveston to seek work. They settled in Galveston and, with the help of the Willis relatives, both found jobs, thus could bring the children to Galveston, reuniting the family.

Richard 11was recalled into the Army Reserve in 1939. He went to Washington, D.C. to attend The Army Industrial College. The family first joined him there, then when Col. Willis was sent, first to Europe, then to China. Genevieve and the children returned to Galveston. Richard 111, the oldest son, joined the Air Force in 1944. Jane, the daughter married in May, 1946. Genevieve and Willie, their youngest son, joined Col. Willis in Yokohama, Japan. By 1948 the family was back in Houston. That same year their daughter Jane took her own life.

In 1954 Richard 11 paid the back taxes on 40 acres of land in Montgomery County that had been part of his grandfather's estate.. They built a house on the property and Richard and Genevieve lived there until he died May 11, 1968. He is buried in Montgomery. Genevieve continued to live in the cabin for a while, later moving to a retirement home in Galveston. She died April 5th, 1993 at age 87. Perhaps it was because she had shared a similar fate as a child and had worked at one time as a social worker, or because of her caring nature, Genevieve Willis took a particular interest in the orphaned Martin children. Genevieve's mother died when she was ten. Her father disappeared for a year. She lived as a foster child in the home of a family friend. Eventually Genevieve's father sent her away to boarding schools – El Paso School For Girls and Manhattenville Convent, Madams of the Sacred Heart in New York City.

In the years that they lived in Galveston the two Willis boys visited in Montgomery, forming a lasting friendship with the Martin boys, especially John, hunting, fishing, riding horses, etc. In return the three little Martin girls were invited to Galveston for visits. I have great memories of their big old house with high ceilings with ceiling fans, a black cook who made delicious meals, riding the roller coaster and going to the beach every day. I especially remember going to dinner one night at Cousin Margaret Sealy Burton's house. I was seated next to her and was fascinated by the little bell she had under the dining table that she could press with her foot and the maid would pop in from the kitchen, and then for dessert she served Baked Alaska---both awesome to a little girl from the country.

It was Genevieve who convinced the guardian of the children to send the three younger Martin girls away to boarding school. Upon hearing of her death, I wrote a note to Richard, her son, expressing my gratitude for the interest his mother had taken in us, the Martin children, and the influence she had on our lives. Richard replied, saying his mother was "his best friend". Turns out she was ours, too.

MAJOR R. S. WILLIS

HENRY HAWLEY WILLIS
MARIAN BROCK

Henry inherited the Willis genes, smaller in statue, much more reserved by nature, and very steady in his progress through life, achieving some success and recognition in his profession.

After Stanton Military School Henry went to work as a roustabout in the oil fields. He then took a cattle boat to San Juan, Puerto, Rico. In 1939 he was living with his mother at the Madison Hotel in New York City. In 1932 he married Marion Brock and settled on Long Island. Their son, William Carter Willis, was born in 1934. Over the years Mamie lived with them periodically. Henry worked for a petroleum company and was sent to India and Japan, his family joining him. Upon retirement they returned to the states, and were last known to be living in Florida. He visited Galveston and Montgomery in 1979.

CHAPTER 7

7th Generation

—

NARCISSA WILLIS MARTIN
JOHN WILLIS MARTIN
I.L. "PETE" MARTIN, JR.
MARY JOSEPHINE MARTIN
ROSE MARIE MARTIN
OLIVE ELIZABETH MARTIN

RICHARD SHORT WILLIS III
WILLIAM EDWARD WILLIS

WILLIAM CARTER WILLIS

"OUR LIVES ARE SHAPED AS much by those who leave as they are by those who stay. Loss is our legacy, insight is our gift, memory is our guide".
From MOTHERLESS DAUGHTERS, The Legacy of Loss by Hope Edelman.